UFOs To Assist "dus"
of Human Set

Project World
Evacuation

Compiled through Tuella
by the
Ashtar Command

Inner Light Publications

Editorial Direction
& Layout:
Timothy Green Beckley

Cover Art by Barbara Lynn

Composition and design:
Cross-Country Consultants

For permission to reprint specific portions or to inquire about foreign rights, address request to Inner Light, Box 753, New Brunswick, NJ 08903

Free catalog of books upon request.

Contents

Dedication

This book is lovingly dedicated to all of the members of the "Intergalactic Legion of Special Volunteers" now present upon this planet.

—**Tuella**

About The Author—Tuella

Tuella's "calling" as a Messenger of Light began in the early seventies with her channeling work commissioned personally by Ashtar on behalf of the Intergalactic Space Confederation. In addition to *Project World Evacuation,* her future works  to be published by Inner Light include *Messengers For The Coming Decade, Ashtar—A Tribute, On Earth Assignment,* and *The Dynamics of Cosmic Telepathy.*

Preface

Just as many are called and few are chosen, likewise, many who read this book will neither understand nor receive the information. But those special souls for whom it is intended will rejoice in its guidance and accept its timely and imperative revelation.

This information is not entertainment. It is comparable to "sealed orders" given to dedicated volunteers on a strategic mission. It is dispersed to them, compiled for them and will be cherished by them. It is neither defended nor justified. It is data recorded as given and passed on to those for whom it is intended.

We are pleased to welcome to these pages in a sharing experience, the words of other beloved messengers who serve the intergalactic Fleets. The many informative and clarifying contributions of "Lucien" (Lucy Colson), Johnnie Prochaska, "Lyara," and Winfield Brownell, are deeply appreciated in filling out the theme.

If your inner truth identifies you as a volunteer from another realm or world on an assignment to Earth, these words are for you. If you are persuaded you are one of the "Star People," you will read this volume with awareness and clarity. If you are a disciple or initiate of the Higher Revelation, you will discern and perceive the purpose of this message from other dimensions of being. If you are a growing, glowing Christian, just beginning to look up and outward beyond the walls of man-made divisions of earthly ecclesiastical hierarchies, your heart will witness to these things. If you are not consciously any of these, read not to scoff, but to hold these revelations in your heart while you "wait and see."

As Elisha prayed that other eyes might be opened to see—and eyes were opened, "to behold the mountains filled with horses and chariots of fire all around Elisha"—so do I fervently call that your vision, as well, be lifted up and expanded, as if by a miracle, to perceive that our planet is "compassed about with such a great cloud of witnesses."

Mission completed,
Tuella

Tuella, author of *Project World Evacuation* and channel for the Ashtar Command.

Foreword

From Jesus the Christ:

"There must be peace on Earth. There must be an end to wars and hatred between brothers. The millions that come from other worlds, from far-off galaxies to assist in bringing Peace upon Earth, have My staunch support and backing for all of their endeavors. They have come IN MY NAME and they serve under My Banner, as Lord of this Planet. They come not as intruders nor usurpers of My Authority, but in loving subjection to the Spiritual Hierarchy of this Solar System, and the Divine Plan for mankind, the deliverance from bondage that has long held humanity in subjection to darkness and sorrow.

"This shall be no more, for these come as My Angels, to reap that which has been sown, to divide and set asunder the tares from the wheat, to gather the wheat into My Barn. For I AM the householder who cometh at the end of the day for an account from His Servants, and to give to all men justly in the manner given by them to Me. So judgment must come; divisions and sorrows must come, but the Earth shall survive all of its totterings. The Just shall inherit the New Earth and the Meek shall know the joy therein.

"I AM SANANDA, KNOWN TO YOU AS JESUS THE CHRIST. I speak in the Authority of My Name and My Office, and I say to you that in the multitudes of the people of the Earth there shall be found that remnant who can steadfastly be faithful to those right principles of my teaching. Those who come In My Name go from heart to heart, sealing them against that day and marking them for deliverance and safety from all that would destroy. But you shall NOT be taken out of your physical forms, but you shall be spared to live on in those days that follow. So, I shall call unto those who follow Me, to listen to the voices of these who come from other worlds, and harden not your hearts against their words nor practices. Rather, lift up LOVE unto them and desire for their coming, for THEY ARE THE ANGELS OF THE HARVEST!

"I AM SANANDA, AND THIS IS MY MESSAGE TO THE WORLD."

Introduction

In time of war upon the Earth, a shrill siren is used to alert the populace that danger is approaching and that they should retire themselves to a place of shelter immediately. We of the Interplanetary Alliance and Space Commands of this hemisphere, known collectively as the Ashtar Command, do now, with the sending forth of this book, sound the siren of warning to mankind.

Danger is upon you. Drop everything and prepare yourselves. It is time to run toward the shelter of Divine Love and Guidance and to take with you only that which you can carry within the inner citadel of being. The early times of this decade will see the fulfillment of all the prophecies that have been released to the world.

Down through many cultures, and century after century, we have permitted our Highest and Brightest of souls to come to you and walk amongst you, to teach, to lift and become your friends. You have been taught many things, shown many things, awakened step by step to a higher way of life, an elevated approach to life, and a better way of existence. Precept upon precept, we have lifted you from one level to another.

Many have benefited and have arisen from their darkness and followed that Light. These have intuitively known that the summons was a call to know themselves and thereby, to undertake that refining of themselves that would reveal the inner divinity. Others have turned their interest elsewhere, ignored the outstretched hand of God, and lifetime after lifetime of opportunity has been squandered by detrimental choices.

Now it is time to separate these groups in keeping with their choices, and let those who refuse the advancement of their being remain together according to their own desires. The few who have burned within their hearts to find the Ultimate Reality will be permitted to follow these aspirations in the setting of a New World, cleansed and made bright by Universal action.

Increasingly, we have noticed the tendency of the planet and its people to pull toward an influence designed to destroy the function of free thinking and freedom of man in making his own choices, governing himself, and managing his national affairs.

This diabolical influence has penetrated wholly within every phase of human life and every avenue of world diplomacy and world statesmanship. Predictably, day by day, the freedom of humanity has been infiltrated with that kind of propaganda which ultimately leads mankind away from their pure heritage as sons of God.

The resulting effects are seen not only in the lives of men, but within the asteroid belt and the planet itself. When humanity stands free, in the full Light of God's Universal Law, all government will be "of the people and for the people and by the people." But when the heritage of freedom is destroyed, mankind becomes as puppets on strings, stripped of honor, life, strength, forthrightness and glory!

The Heavenly Father has placed within the burning center of man that likeness of Himself which enables man to govern himself in righteousness and peace. The destruction of this center has been the goal of the Destroyer. Now the forces of Light and Righteousness must rise in the defense of humanity before it is too late. This is the primary action taking place behind the visible scene surrounding all of life.

Now, all levels of life will be highly raised in frequency, and all manifestations of lower life will wither and dissolve and be removed from the visible scene, to reconstruct the Father's Plan for this beautiful planet. A new fresh start for man is in the making! The astral belts will be purged, the heavens will be cleared, the nature kingdom will find its true destiny and humanity will be glorified in keeping with the Father's design. This is coming to pass in your generation. There is no time left to dally and consider. The hour of decision for a planet is not only come, it is almost gone.

So it is, the "siren sounds" for mankind, and there is silence in heaven for that moment that now is, when this great separation shall take place. You who read are versed in the spiritual verities involved. This book will clarify human consciousness concerning the future on your octave. Read...and understand.

The Ashtar Command

PART I

The Seven Secret Councils

The New Strategy

It was very late. The day had ended. Silently the darkness crept in and overshadowed us with its coolness and peace. I gazed, spellbound, at the brilliance of the heaven world, loathe to remove myself from the inner fullness of the moment. I was overcome with a deep love for my friends of outer space.

Suddenly my head was magnetically turned to the right. I sensed someone standing there. Then my head was again magnetically pulled upward to measure the great height of the Being at my side. He requested that I give him my hand, and I did. My hand tingled as if asleep or touching something electrically charged. I began to sense the presence of many other Beings surrounding me. Their heads were bowed in prayer. I realized they were standing very close together, actually forming a circle. I then became aware that they were holding both of my hands and that I was a part of the closely-knit circle. Together we all became a glorious beam of white-golden Light. When the prayer ended, someone appeared in the circle standing directly in front of me with hands extended in blessing. The Being before me was in a jumpsuit type of garment, in shiny metallic-like material with a type of hood that fits close to the head. His eyes were clear blue, and it seemed he was smiling at me.

"I will speak with you now, Tuella. I am Ashtar. I will remove my hood so that you may perceive my appearance. (His shoulder length light blonde hair fell straight back from her forehead and down.) Yes, I am smiling at you, Tuella, in my

14

love for your spiritual being. You are glowing tonight because of the love you have been feeling. Because of this shedding forth and giving out of the love within, you have created a shining vortex surrounding you, and I am standing within it in a projection of my Being. This is done mentally, just as my words are beamed to you mentally. Hold the projection of my appearance before you as I continue with my message for this evening." Thus began the various discourses which make up this text.

Ashtar is a Beloved Christian Commander and a very beautiful Being. He is highly evolved in the upper worlds, very influential, and has a great benefactoring influence upon those he leads. The momentum of the vibrations from these Great Space Beings, or Commanders, as they call themselves, is equal to and often beyond the force-field even of Ascended Masters, for many have come who are Lords on their own planet, or persons of highest repute in their own galaxies and dimensions. We must realize that the fact that a Being is a participating Commander within the Confederation of planets does not lessen in any way his or her spiritual evolvement and ascension within his or her own lifestream. Ashtar and those who serve with him are as real as you or I. In the Alliance of the Space Confederation, Commander Ashtar is the highest in authority for our hemisphere. He is also the Commander of the star ship upon which our Beloved Lord and Great Commander, Jesus-Sananda, spends so much of His time. He has the authority to clear any channel and interrupt and take over any communication from any source at any time, upon our planet; yet he is gentle, loving, devout, and totally inspiring as a great leader.

I was told that this book will trigger into action many yet outside of this awareness and that the Intergalactic Fleets would take up the work from that momentum in establishing these key souls on their pathway and personal mission. Further, that "all emissaries now in embodiment will be assisted immediately to fulfill the divine plan for their lives." Many who will read the book are "Ambassadors" from the far-flung vistas of outer space, having volunteered to endure the limitations of fleshly existence that they might in some way aid the coming of Light upon this planet. It was explained to me that within the vast army of volunteers, there is an inner circle of souls on very special missions of great responsibility to the others, like a circle within a circle. In cosmic circles, these are referred to as the "Intergalactic Legion of Special Volunteers."

It seems that mankind must make a new adjustment of attitude toward these intermediaries between Earth and Heaven. The Commands plead for mankind to accept them, their existence, their presence, their dedication and loyalty to the Confederation and devotion to Earth, that the Kingdom of God shall come and that Earth shall become a beautiful sun and part of the united heavens. They are telling us now that, "our special representatives must be lifted, taught, and prepared to fulfill their part in the plan for rescuing the planet and its people."

The opening message goes as follows:

"I am Ashtar, the Commander of ten million men surrounding this hemisphere in the protective force within the Alliance for Peace in the Intergalactic Council. We have called upon this messenger to compile this book for this point in earth time that mankind might consider and understand the details of those things that could come to pass, for Our Father doeth nothing except first He warneth His prophets.

"There is method and great organization in a detailed plan already near completion for the purpose of removing souls from this planet, in the event of catastrophic events making a rescue necessary. We watch diligently, the threat of a polar shift for the planet in your generation. Such a development would create a planetary situation through which none could survive. This would necessitate an evacuation such as I have referred to.

"Another manifestation necessitating global rescue would be the collision of an asteroid within your own magnetic field, or the bypass of another solar system. This would so disrupt and disturb your own grid system and energy field that all of the inhabitants of the planet would face extinction. The negativity of man could magnetize these things to himself. Detailed scientific data accumulated over long periods of monitoring the actions of the bodies within the solar system indicates these events are within the realm of possibility.

"This book is not intended to frighten anyone, but on the contrary, to hold out the hope and confidence of our presence with you for any time of trouble. The dangers to the planet are very real. The resulting tragedy to humanity would be unavoidable. However, our presence surrounding you thirty-five million strong will assist you, lift you up and rescue you, and hold you in safety.

"The magnetized solar flares now present around the sun in its position, in conjunction with the planetary alignment that is presently coming into its final position, combines to create a strong tendency to pull the Earth into untoward motion. The possible polar shift has been greatly lessened and gentled by the action of our scientific volunteers from many worlds. These are greatly learned men who understand these things, and whose services have gladly been given for the purpose of saving this beautiful planet. There are also tracking units with the Ashtar Command which continually trace the pathways of all asteroid action within this solar system and beyond. Any threatening approach of another heavenly body can be strongly averted from its direction. This type of surveillance is constant.

"Inner disturbances taking place within the planet itself are direct recollections of the aspirations and the attitudes and vibrations of those who dwell upon it. We have repeatedly attempted to turn the thoughts of humanity toward the reality of Divine Truth and Principles. We have dared to lower our craft into your frequencies in a visible way. We have dared to expose ourselves in vulnerable situations in order to convince

17

souls of Earth of our presence.

"Now we take further steps, because of the shortness of time and the dangers that beset you and the pressure of coming events. We come to you once again with our call and our warning, but this time WE DARE to expose our most secret strategy to sound the alarm that this is indeed the midnight hour. Now is the time to inventory the inner values. Therefore, we dare to expose within the pages of this book, our plans to come out into the open and send proof of our presence and existence back to the Earth to silence forever arguments and denials of our overshadowing protection. This is the new strategy unveiled to you at this time in exposing our proposed gatherings of those who have come to walk among you as our representatives. They have to work in service to you, and we dare to reveal them and their identities, for no harm can come to them. We would simply remove them from your midst if you were to attempt to harm them in any way.

"They are citizens of your planet, who have lived with you, suffered with you, walked with you and truly been one of you. Now we call them forth to admit their identity, to be gathered together to spend a brief time with us that they might return to you and share with you the facts and the proofs of our existence and the truth of our words.

"The Ashtar Command now sends forth this book, that you, oh men of Earth, might be forewarned that these things shall take place. As these are gathered with us and returned once again into your midst, you will know that the events described in these councils are also true. You will know that global evacuation will take place. You will be helped and you will be rescued and by the proofs that are given our representatives who return to you, you will know that our promises are true.

"We leave this book upon the planet for the few who will accept it. These words are not for the many, but for those to whom they are sent; more importantly, that later, those who

18

remain behind will know why they have not been taken. Let all read and be quickened in the inner levels of being!"

* * *

Closely following the message from Ashtar, my own teacher, Kuthumi, also discussed these things:

"Those who have come to your world and taken upon themselves the garment of flesh to serve the planet in Our Name, are approaching a time of crisis. These have chosen to be present upon Terra to serve in the great harvest of souls that now comes, To these, many instructions must be given, and many discussions sent to them to be assimilated within their guidance systems. Now is the hour when these special emissaries are to be temporarily removed from Terra for a brief moment of time, to receive specialized training instructions and personal directives, that they may be clothed in preparedness for the times that are at hand! The latter portion of this fateful year could bring many upheavals and disturbances to the physical level of your planet.

"Planetary changes have already taken place on inner levels within the auric field and the astral belt and surrounding regions. Soon, these emanations will penetrate the physical octave and those who dwell thereon. We have prepared the hearts and souls of incarnate humanity in our own manner, for the coming events. It is imperative that our special emissaries under Hierarchal authority to participate in planetary evacuation, now receive our attention, by focusing our efforts toward their thorough preparation for the mission ahead.

"Several million universal volunteers now walk the Earth! They are filled with Light, complete in their dedication and consecration to serve the Celestial Government, the Solar Hierarchy and the Intergalactic Confederation, in the salvation of a planet. The Highest Celestial Councils have decreed that those chosen ones shall be personally removed from Earth, to be temporarily placed in a higher frequency, within our domain,

19

and there be prepared spiritually for the mission to be completed.

"The planet Earth is tottering upon a crisis of many changes. The input of direct energies from many sources, now whirling clockwise fashion around the globe, has been set into motion to offset a multitude of inner earth actions now racing toward chaos on the outer crust of the sphere. Because of these inner convulsions of energy within the orb of Terra that now press toward their destiny upon the crust, we must immediately organize our special training efforts for those assigned to these emergencies.

"Therefore, I send forth this alert and summons to our Elect, to be ready for a sudden removal for a brief time to be spent in the presence of those who guard the planet. They will receive special instruction and directives to hide within their being. Many have been called, but few have been chosen, and to those a very special training now awaits. It is true that much teaching and much training and preparation has taken place before entering the human manifestation. It is also true that these have proven their loyalty and love to the Father many times over. Every chosen disciple and initiate participating in this great rescue program must now consciously imbibe details, directions, and specifics through the human consciousness. The summons may come through personal guidance, through the word of another, through this book, or through a lecture perhaps, but be assured your call will be given and heard. Then you must organize the details of your lives to be ready for withdrawal from your personal situations for a period of approximately 14 to 21 days for purposes I have outlined.

"The interim of waiting for your summons should be a time of personal discipline, assimilating information, and bypassing worldly activities which rob one's spiritual strength and power. Saturate your inner being with the spiritual vibrations that interact with your own energy field. Meditate upon the needs of humanity and the power of the Light of God to meet those needs. Let this interim be a time of great expectations, of deep soul searching and counting tee cost,

"You remain free to withdraw your original commitment to this mission, under the concept of free will. Beloved sons and daughters of the Light, the choice is still your own. You will receive reward and gratitude for work accomplished thus far. If that mind be in you to carry on and continue the battle against darkness through your dedication to the Legions of Light, your blessings shall be unlimited. You shall be highly protected and specially annointed with gifts such as are necessary for your personal service to mankind.

"I am Kuthumi, World Teacher, and my own emanations and vibrations surround every world volunteer at this hour. I cover you with my Golden Cloak, and I charge your being on inner levels to hold fast to your crown and to steadfastly remain faithful to your pledge. Realize that a great cloud of powerful Beings surrounds you and exalts your calling and giveth you grace equal to the task. Others who speak after me will introduce the details of our plan. I shed forth my love and blessing to all who have determined to serve as 'ground forces' in this tremendous undertaking. My beloved brothers and sisters, initiates of the Golden Light, not one of you shall fall; not one of you shall be lost; not one of you will be touched by the Destroyer! None shall fail in your choice to complete the Mission, and not one of you shall be plucked from the Father's Hand! Beloved ones, you are the Light of the World in its darkest hour for this cycle of time. Stand in our places. Stand firm in your consecration until the hour is come. Blessings be upon you in the Name of Our Radiant One. So be it."

As I considered these messages, I realized that the intimacy of the silence and its unspeakable fellowship helps us more and more to comprehend the Master's statement, "It is given unto you to know the mysteries of the kingdom of heaven, but to them it is not given." Only because our "hall of learning" is the inner citadel, the secret place of the Most High! I say, go inward, man, in your quest of that which you cannot find in the churches of the world. If you are blind, let not the blind lead thee. He "madest us to have dominion over the works of His Hands, and hast put all things under our feet." Believe it! Hold fast to your spiritual heritage as the begotten of God. In the days of Noah, eight close souls were saved because they had prepared an ark of safety and listened within the inner citadel to the Voice of God. They believed His words and followed His instructions.

* * *

Further insight into the new strategy of the Space Confederation came in a message from Andromeda Rex, one who will become a very familiar Ambassador of Light on television and radio, broadcasting warnings to the people. He states:

"The gathering of our ground Commanders for these secret council meetings will begin a new way of doing things by the Confederation. Hitherto, we have had to be coy and careful and subdued in our activities. But now we are prepared to be more outward in manifestation and bolder in our efforts to win the hearts of mankind to our cause and purpose, which is really their own. This is why those who are taken up to these seven secret gatherings will be permitted to bring back with them so much evidential material. We will allow our participants to be interviewed and quizzed by the curious, because only in this way can we be heard and vindicated. This is a brave thing we ask of all of you. We are aware of the temptations involved to vaunt the self for such widespread attention. Yet we have chosen you well, and we believe none shall be spoiled by any of these developments but shall hold steady in the consecration previously made. All of you have been thoroughly scrutinized and monitored, down to the most minute detail of your inner being and personality traits. This was done before our final choices were made, to carry on and complete this program which began one hundred years ago.

22

"Soon, now, with much joy in our hearts, we will once again send back down into Earth those whom we have, by their own election, chosen to prepare the planet for its initiation into a new field of expression with the rest of the solar system. In the annointing that is to be given at the inaugural ceremony, signs and wonders will be bestowed for convincing the world, each receiving in accordance with the mission, whatever is needed to complete it. We have designated certain areas of the ships where your cameras will operate successfully. Your tape recorders will also operate normally with batteries only. Primarily there will be many items of interest which can be brought back with you as evidences. THESE COUNCILS, OR GATHERINGS, AS YOU HAVE BEGUN TO CALL THEM, ARE PRIMARILY FOR THIS PURPOSE OF SENDING BACK TO EARTH THE CONCRETE EVIDENCE WHICH EARTH HAS SO LONG CLAMORED FOR. You will also have photographs to return with you which will show the views of Earth taken from our ships, taken upon our highly evolved technical equipment—photos which cannot be denied.

"All of those who are summoned to these briefings will in some manner be linked together to assist each other in the overall project of evidential presentation. Thus, there will be those from media, from commerce, from messenger work, and from church groups. Each will be a coordinated group, who will be made known to each other for coordinating your efforts toward convincing unbelievers of our existence and our good intentions. This program is designed for the purpose of convincing mankind, as well as the training of those who attend. Thus, with the books that will be written and the efforts of higher echelons to protect those books and those writers, this will be an all-out onslaught against ignorance and bigotry as it pertains to us, our presence, and our mission.

"The ranks of the officers will be revealed, specific missions will be assigned as this last phase of the transition period will be underway and soon to be completed. This legion of special volunteers will be the most active on inner levels to initiate the preparedness for our coming into Earth's atmosphere. Commander Ashtar and many others will address the groups and explain the mission of each one present so that all can hear and know the direction that each individual will take. This program is a crucial step in our gearing down. All details for each personal life and its related problems or complications will be clearly discussed and dealt with in private council. Some of our guests will need much calming, for many will be lifted up rather suddenly from the midst of their affairs, creating some internal anxiety. It will be the work of all of you and us to calm such as these.

"We are naturally tremendously thrilled over this coming fellowship, as well as our new policy and program. Our last effort of fifty years ago and later, did not succeed as we had hoped. It was to have culminated with our full and open appearance in your skies. This should have occurred in the sixties had our past programs proceeded as planned, but the hindrances and hostility of the governments of Earth totally thwarted our original plans.

"We do not desire to force our presence upon you, and thereby feed the negative nature of those who would oppose us. This would gain us nothing toward Interplanetary Fellowship. We CANNOT, we WILL NOT make our appearance (in normal times) unless it is accepted by the military and higher branches of your governments. Therefore, this new policy of inner penetration into human hearts will hopefully achieve that necessary change in the policies of mankind which will build us a platform of goodwill upon which we may make our approach to uplift your way of life.

"It must be done peacefully and lovingly, while it CAN be done in that manner. If circumstances develop danger to the Elect and danger to the solar system before these negotiations are completed, then we will be forced circumstantially to intrude ourselves into Earth's force-field for evacuation and intervention in the name of the Intergalactic Council governing the Universal Peace agreement.

"I am Andromeda Rex, and I speak this message on behalf of the entire Space Confederation and the Council of Universal Masters who serve the Divine Government."

* * *

As we think together of a vast army of volunteers to Earth for this crucial time, our understanding is penetrated by these words of Cosmic Being, LYTTON, which came to spiritual messenger "Lyara":

"Each of you who is attuned to this material has a mission of service to mankind. Each of you, as sparks of God, is a divine and unique ray of the Father. Cosmic family members have already achieved mastery and forms of advancement in other dimensions, realms and/or realities and are reawakening this dormant knowledge. You each agreed, in coming here, to be veiled, that you could adjust and understand the people of this planet to better serve them. Some of you have been here several times—very few more than that. All of you have awakened, or will, to the realization that the home you are most clearly attuned to is not resemblant of Earth. Planets where you have spent the most time and call home are higher vibrating and have all-pervading auras of Christ Love. All you belong to the Intergalactic Fleet. At debriefing time before embarking on this mission, you realized only to some degree the hazards that you would experience on this planet. The most serious was not preparing yourself to wake up, by getting involved and caught up with Earth's activities and pleasures and forgetting your identity. many brothers and sisters have not yet awakened sufficiently to fulfill their missions in the remaining time allotted. It has made for many adjustments in plans, and many others of you will be asked to assume greater responsibilities than originally contracted for. We realize it will cause some hardships and extra burdens, but by staying

25

attuned to your guidance, these new assignments which are being asked of you in the Father's name can still be expressions of joy. Allow your spirits to soar while your feet are on the ground for planetary functioning."

It is my understanding that these veils are to be lifted at the gatherings. Mary Hardy, well known for her family's research on pyramidology, made this interesting statement recently in an article appearing in the New Atlantean Journal: "When an individual is taken up into a ship, the electromagnetic field (aura) around the body is accelerated. In this field there is no time. An individual can learn the future or the past. Space craft are designed to accelerate the particles that make up the atom. These particles can travel up to 27 times faster than the known speed of light.

This change of frequency is why ships become invisible. The individual inside the ship can travel time and can look into the future or the past. At the end of the trip these individuals are DE-accelerated, or decelerated. They are placed in a chair or on a light-emitting table and brought back to a stable frequency attuned to the Earth."

The Summons to the Secret Councils

During January of 1982 I received a message from Andromeda Rex which clearly shows the groundwork being initiated in preparation for these meetings, stressing the need and importance of "networking" between the factions of Light on Earth:

"The Commands are sending forth an extra power to those whose vibrations can handle the higher frequencies. We will now be stepping up all of those who are capable, to their highest capacity. The trembling of body you are presently experiencing is an incidental aspect of this accelerated frequency. We are all alerted and geared up for a massive sweep of power to accentuate all Light frequencies upon the planet. A tremendous input of Light through beam radiation is now being undertaken for purposes of quickening the Light bodies of all who can receive it. This action tends to be one preparation for that which is to come later.

"There is also underway a great spiritual urgency toward the integration of Light souls toward each other. We are attempting through these higher frequencies to draw Light Workers closer together in feeling and purpose. The networking objective is going on successfully. We are attempting to create a CONSCIOUS NETWORK of Light Beings in embodiment, that will be CONSCIOUSLY entered into and CONSCIOUSLY COOPERATED WITH for purposes that will

27

come later. This CONSCIOUS linking of souls is most important to our objective in preparing for mass intervention if events warrant this action.

"The NETWORK, CONSCIOUSLY accepted, becomes a great force for the ongoing of our program toward the rescue of, and assistance to, the planet. Even in New Age circles there must be a falling away of technical differences and an emphasis upon things on which there is agreement. Regardless of the particular slant or emphasis of truth, there must be a CONSCIOUS desire to become a link in the great chain of ground forces rather than to stand alone. It is this CONSCIOUS desire to be a CONSCIOUS OPERATING portion of the whole, that will create the proper atmosphere for the uplifting of frequencies I have described.

"Therefore, let all of those who serve with us strive toward this holy attitude of ONENESS with each other, that we might all function together as one great beam of Light upon the Earth. This effort toward united purpose is the present focus of our interaction with our brothers and sisters of Light now in human embodiment. In this Great Cosmic Light, I salute you all. I am Andromeda Rex."

In times past, in our progressive enlightenment and spiritual perception, we have seen only a part, "as through a glass darkly;" but now, as the networking expands and the veils ARE being lifted, we "know, even as we are known." The joyful quickening as one soul recognizes another, warmed by the Christ Presence within the other—that quickening is now manifesting even "face to face" as well as between this and the highest dimensions of reality. There is an unconscious network between us all on the inner level Universe, but Andromeda would have us pull this reality through our human consciousness, having used the word eight different times to make his point. He describes these things further: "These gatherings represent a highly momentous occasion. There has never yet been anything like this in the history of mankind's sojourn upon the planet. Similar incidents have fragmentarily taken place in isolated cases far between, in the past and last generation, but nothing on so large a scale, so thoroughly organized as this venture. Neither were the former results that far-reaching, yet there has been a tremendous secret penetration in the past forty years. But following these secret council meetings and the return of the Elect to their octave, there will be an immediate saturation of all the news media and worldwide recognition of those who have thus been honored by this encounter. This will be one of the greatest news stories ever written.

"The program will be a very detailed briefing of coming events which will set up and coordinate our ground forces in a very specific manner while outlining levels of authority and responsibilities. Our key Commanders, now incarnate, will be introduced to each other and the fellowship will be a precious experience. The marshalling of all of our forces for this undertaking which is so important to the Hierarchal Program, has been a tremendous challenge and one in which thousands have beautifully cooperated."

* * *

I was visiting in Utah for a week in June. On the day of the June 21st eclipse, it was announced to me that this book was to begin immediately. A typewriter was borrowed and for the four remaining days there, the dictations came at a pace of four a day. Commander Ashtar spoke forcefully on the day of the eclipse:

"We desire to speak to our people. We desire to speak to the Elect of God who have chosen and been chosen to come as volunteers from out of our midst to walk the Earth, to endure the darkness and the challenges and the problems, yea, the temptations; yet to stand and be ready when our call comes to them. As Commander, it is my desire to speak to all of these throughout this hemisphere, as messengers, as teachers, as guidance counselors, as channels of Light and beams of the

Love of God to the planet. We have need now to lift you into our presence for a brief moment of time for purposes of special training and many other matters which cannot be handled in any other way. These gatherings shall not be simultaneous throughout the globe, but shall take place in seven various sectors, one at a time. We cannot dispense our forces efficiently by having all of you at once. Therefore, we shall undertake this program in units, by areas, as we have organized other programs in the past.

"We are attempting to streamline our program so that the time can be shortened. We have prepared our facilities with great care and outlined our agenda very carefully so that the utmost efficiency in all of these things may be applied.

"One of the most important elements within all of this activity is that you would become personally acquainted with each other in a network of sharing the knowledge of the mission of each member. One might call you a 'secret army,' so to speak, for you are an army in spiritual warfare, and in most cases, your activity will be in secret. Nevertheless, a vast portion of the program will not be in secret, but rather, deliberately publicized as a part of our strategy, and details concerning that strategy have already been delivered to this messenger to be incorporated into the text of this material.

"I am assured by the officers under my Command who represent the various units and areas of this hemisphere for which I am responsible; I am assured by these that almost all of the Earth representatives are now ready in their awareness to be taken into our presence without undue adjustments or misalignments or misunderstanding, and that we may now carry on with our plans to fulfill this enormous project. I am Ashtar, of the star ship upon which our Beloved Commander, Sananda, travels and calls His home away from home, although of course, this great Avatar is capable of being anywhere and everywhere simultaneously.

"Within the network of our Commands and the Galactic

Confederation, we have an interlocking communications system through which every individual craft may at any given moment receive a certain transmission simultaneously. In many cases when one of you is in an act of service or some victory for the Light is occurring, reports of these are instantaneously sent throughout the hemisphere and the entire spiritual hierarchy. It is impossible for you to conceive the speed with which our communications go forth throughout the entire universe.

"I can absolutely assure you that your reception of our message when the alert has come, will be received. We are capable of entering the thought patterns of any individual upon the planet and implanting there our impressions in keeping with Universal Law, clearly and decisively. Each and every one of you who is on Earth assignment to be a part of this program will receive clear signals and a message that cannot be mistaken nor misunderstood.

"Whatever your past experiences in telepathic communication have been, or your progress in conscious awareness of these revelations, you will receive our message loud and clear. You will be personally approached either by one of us, or be told by one who represents us. Do not make any moves or changes or hesitate when this is received. By the same token, do not take any action along these lines if these or one of these is not received. Do not be concerned nor unduly upset if you do not participate in this first temporary lift-up of souls who serve with us. This merely means that your action in the plan is elsewhere, and you will be taken for your instructions or will receive them in some other manner. Do not take any personal affront if you are not alerted or are not a participant in this first phase of our plan. Your time will come later, and these instructions are not necessary for you at this time.

"We are bringing together those of high leadership status whose responsibilities are far reaching, and of such a nature that special instructions and training must be given if they are to fulfill their portion of the mission. These have long been in

31

accord with us on inner levels and have spent much time in coordinating necessary discussions relating to their missions while out of body in their night visits with our councils. All of these have sat in on our council meetings while their bodies have slept. Each of you who are to be lifted up in this special gathering have all participated in intergalactic and interplanetary council meetings and listened to preparedness programs. This meeting, in our presence, will take place upon a conscious level. You will retain your full consciousness at every moment and at all times. On this visit you will take with you when you return to Earth situations, a full recall of all that has transpired, along with many evidences of where you have been. Each one of you will be able to prove your sojourn with us, for each will receive undeniable proof to combine with the testimony of many others throughout the globe, presenting accounts consistent with your own. You will be given two objects—one to wear, and one to hold—that will anchor you to that moment for the rest of this embodiment.

"You will return to your earthly situations with a quiet spiritual authority that will never be taken from you and will never forsake you. You will be annointed with spiritual credentials and spiritual abilities representing your badge of initiation and mission. At first, your words will be scoffed at and your reports will bring laughter to the multitudes. But all over the world you will stand together, united in your story, consistent in your report, agreeing in your details, and you will cause them to remove the smiles from their countenances when your credentials are activated. You are the representatives of the Highest Celestial Government and the Highest Council of this solar system, as well as the Highest Tribunal of the Interplanetary Councils.

"All of us will reinforce each and every one of you, and you will be convinced of this before you leave our midst to return.

"There are so many of you presently to be lifted, trained

and prepared. It is a project of such magnitude that words can scarcely describe not only the effort thus far invested into it over many centuries, but also, the great labor and the millions of volunteers that make it possible.

"Therefore, my closing words to my beloved brothers and sisters of Light in this message is a salute to you in the sign of the Solar Cross. I hold forth my right hand of blessing upon each of you. You know who you are. You know where you stand in your places and your inner guidance. Unfortunately, our words and messages will confuse many, but those who must hear will hear; and those who must see will see. To him that hath ears to hear, let him hear; to him that hath eyes to see, let him see. So be ready, my brethren. Be alert. Be listening, for your call shall come. I am Ashtar, one who commands millions of men in this hemisphere for our Beloved Commander in Chief, Jesus the Christ and the World Saviour."

* * *

On my return to New Mexico, the pressure continued to mount to get into the book, even to a grand upheaval in my personal affairs within a matter of days. When I "came up for breath" from a greatly accelerated and disturbing chain of events, I grumbled to one of my venerable Brothers, "You guys play kind of rough!" Ignoring my vernacular, his counter comment is memorable:

"You have given us permission to act and to create for and with you in the events of your life. It is correct that we do not involve ourselves in the smaller details in the life of an earthly volunteer, knowing full well that they have the discernment and the ability to arrange their lives and their affairs for the best. But it is also true that all of the details of Earth-based Commanders' lives touch their mission, as they touch their lives. So consider these things within the framework of permission previously given for intervention. You see, Tuella, many eons ago, you gave us that permission to direct the circumstances of your life in that manner which would best facilitate the mission for which you have come." Perhaps that reply will help the understanding of another.

At any rate, I suddenly found myself in a situation where almost full time could be devoted to this labor, in a setting of withdrawal and perfect solitude. It has been said that the mills of the gods grind exceedingly small, but in this, our day, they certainly do not grind slowly! The urgency of this volume was continually pressed upon my consciousness. Even in a letter from Lyara, Monka injected this thrust: "Attempt conscious completion in a less professional manner or whatever else is necessary to get this information into people's hands as early as possible. All events are organized with absolute preciseness this year. As you have been receiving the last and final leg of the journey, so it is to be accomplished." With one sweep, his guidance eliminated plans for typesetting and binding procedures, which would have added many weeks to production time. Their aura of urgency became contagious! Grateful for this confirmation, I plunged assiduously into the task!

* * *

Immediately following the conclusion of the July semi-annual Conclave of the Fleets of the southwestern sector of America, Captain Avalon reported to me, advising that the Floridian Command Communications Center had been host for their meeting there, as well as beneath Cook Mountain. All states and areas of the Southwest were represented by their Officers and persons of great responsibilities. The subject receiving the most attention and longest detailed discussion had to do with lift-up and evacuation details of our section. (Attention, reader: these quarterly conclaves take place at all sectors of the globe.) There is to be one more large final meeting to tie all the loose ends of the plan, but it will involve the entire higher echelon of the Commands. It seems they were concerned to make one important distinction. So much material had now piled up, I was having a bit of confusion from it all regarding the various lift-offs and phases, etc.:

"We wish to clarify these matters. Your confusion has ensued in classifying the briefing withdrawal as a phase of the global evacuation. During this training withdrawal, there are not likely to be any global disturbances present. These gatherings are designed as training programs for our Earth-based Commanders. One large element of their responsibilities will be the education of Light workers and their followers. *SPECIAL PROGRAMS FOR REACHING AND EDUCATING THE MASSES HAVE NOW CEASED.* Concentration is directed toward specialized training for the changes ahead.

"Please make this distinction. The very first action will be the lifting of these ground Leaders—the Elect, who bear tremendous responsibilities in their assignments. This is a TEMPORARY withdrawal for a short period of time, and is NOT a lift-off phase of the global evacuation. It is not necessarily a lift-off, since all councils will remain in your atmosphere and locations. This withdrawal does not constitute the 'twinkling of an eye' lift-up of Light Workers which is, in essence, Phase I of the planetary evacuation.

"Therefore, the time sequence calls first for the Commander gatherings to take place as a preparation for the global evacuation steps which will occur quickly or later in the future. The Commander councils may involve some landings in secluded areas."

* * *

With this clarification of the sequence of events, a very informative body of information from Andromeda Rex was received by spiritual messenger Lucy Colson and submitted for this focus. Parts of it are scattered in various sections of the text. Andromeda states:

"The Gatherings will take place under the deepest secrecy imaginable. The 'Gathering of Eagles' will come first. This meeting will consist of the advanced echelon of Commanders, a group of highly trained Beings, skilled in planetary affairs. They will contact world governments, groups of Light students, preparing them for an eventual lift-off while the planet is made new. The people must be advised that this is imminent. Those who will remain behind to pass through the fire and water must know the reasons why they will not be lifted off. For out of this trial will come new leaders and new hope for humanity. They must know that they are never really alone.

"The Earthean Eagles will bring back with them from the meeting, concrete, indisputable proof! The Eagles are the ones who will be needed immediately in the days ahead; and *who will be beamed up last* during evacuation. The Earthean Eagles will be contacted and expected to be at their destined positions in as little time as twelve hours from the time of the Call to Gather. The Eagles will also remain for the regular Gathering, to be briefed with everyone else, and will then brief the Light Commanders under them."

* * *

As I speak with many people, I find evidence that the collective unconscious of the race knows a purging is being initiated, with a significance deeper than that which can be ascribed by them to conventional wisdom. Cosmic Being Lytton, transmitting through spiritual messenger Lyara, speaks of an early fruition of the Divine Plan:

"Great power and forces will be unleashed this year. Major initiations for some. Cleansing of the bodies, veils being lifted, and survival disks being received for those returning for evacuation assignments. Some brothers and sisters will not be receiving these messages. It is not for them to know. Their work is different than yours, and they need to remain on their path. Accelerated energies will be intense. What a few years ago would take years to accomplish will be completed in a day. You will experience continual initiations...."

* * *

During the period when work was underway compiling this manuscript, I received an urgent summons from Captain Avalon, of the Floridian Mountains Communications Center for the Southwest, which is near my home. He informed me that on the Sunday before full moon, a very crucial Council would be in session there. He requested that I present myself at 7:00 a.m. that Sunday morning to record the words of the major speakers.

On the evening before the designated Sunday, I could not refrain from inspecting the atmosphere surrounding the Floridas. With the predictable certainty, there was the usual heavy dark cloud bank totally hiding the upper portion of the mountains and spanning out all over the area. This phenomenon invariably appears when any kind of council is going on there. The dark mist and clouds hovered as expected, until the great Council was concluded.

Promptly at 7:00 on August 1, I had concluded my devotions, and I called him. We had done this type of work together before on two occasions. His response was crisp and prompt:

"Good morning! This is Avalon, responding for my previous appointment. I will tell you what is happening here. A great conclave is taking place this weekend in the great conference hall of our installation beneath the Floridian Mountains. All of the important leaders from every sector of this nation are here, and a few representatives of the Jupiter Command from the other hemisphere, as well. The purpose of this tribunal is to coordinate all of our preparations and to delegate specific assignments that will be delegated within the Commands to each sector, for completing the secret gatherings. Everyone you ever heard of is here, as far as the Alliance goes. Ashtar will appear later today. By the way, these conclaves are always held at or near the full moon period. We feel that it is important to include in your manuscript the text of these messages today, so that your readers may actually hear a planning session in which the Gatherings were discussed. You will be in session for about an hour for the first one, and there will be three or four other sessions today. I have just been told nothing will be happening of significance for an hour, so I will release you until that time. Avalon speaking, and closing the contact."

* * *

An hour later, this striking overview began. Because many details were given to me, I will also share them with you.

"Thank you, Tuella. We are gathered in the great hall, centrally located within and beneath our Communications Center. What an impressive crowd! As you know, we are here to coordinate and finalize plans and specifics for the coming Gatherings. Everyone is in his place, waiting for the Chairman to appear.

"Let me describe the scene to you. Our room is about 150 feet in diameter, round in shape and furnished like an amphitheatre or one of your sports stadiums. The entire circling wall is filled with comfortable seating graduated down in rows, enabling clear vision of the rostrum. The audience chairs are upholstered in red, and the walls give forth radiance everywhere in an overall glow, so that one cannot tell from where it originates. The doors and other openings are not discernible, for they blend into the wall contour, making them invisible until opened. We control these mechanisms with thought, which to you would be the application of crystalline energy. We have a domed ceiling on which beautiful artwork is painted. To you, it would be reminiscent of the ceilings of the Versailles Palace near Paris. However, the subject of our artwork here embraces Universal settings and planetary motions. It is a very beautiful room, and is reserved for only occasions of this level of importance or tribunals of distinction. Soft music of the spheres provides a pleasant background and everyone is watching the area where the speakers will enter.

"The center arena has the usual rostrum in the center, surrounded by a circular table with seating for twelve. These chairs are upholstered in a brilliant blue and beyond them are four sets of three chairs, arranged in triangle placement, to the east, the west, the north, and the south. These chairs are yellow. All chairs in the room are placed within a white circle that is part of the floor design, which is otherwise a solid color. The white circle has a magnetic energy emanating from it to energize the one who sits in the chair. An electronic signal light is built within the arm of each chair for letting the leader know a comment is desired by that participant.

"The opening from the east corridor approach has been opened and the twenty-four dignitaries have entered and taken their places. Commander Ashtar is the Chairman, and he is addressing the audience. You can hear him... please record his words:"

"We are deeply grateful to all of you who have laid aside your busy schedules to answer this call to join this deliberation. We have called up a generous cross section of the leadership from all sectors to blend your thinking with our own on the many problems to be solved. Our Most Beloved Great Commander, Sananda, will be joining us later in the day. The speaker for this morning's session is one of the most respected members of our Commands, having served the Confederation in many capacities and many examples of his great concern for the people of earth. He stands as their protector at this hour, and represents them in our major councils. His words and decisions are of great importance to all of us, and I join with you in earnest attention to his words. I bring toward our friend and brother... Monka!"

Monka Addresses the Great Council

(Monka is seated to the right side of Ashtar's chair. As he rises, the hall bursts with a standing ovation of salutations to Beloved Monka, our great leader).

"Good morning, ladies and gentlemen of the great Commands that circle the Earth. Our fellowship together at this full moon period has a touch of sadness to it, when we consider the purpose for our meeting. None of us can look upon the events in store for planet Earth without that twinge of regret within our being that it might have been different had man responded to the Great Light that was given.

"Nevertheless, we do rejoice together for the many who have made it, and who will carry on the program of the Kingdom of God on Earth when the Earth is made ready.

"I am bringing you this morning, a portion of our findings as we have monitored the Earth population in its ascension toward spiritual unfoldment. There are at least forty million souls now embodied who are our own representatives, or followers of those representatives, who follow our directives and give attention to our words. This group will form the nucleus of the first two phases of evacuation. Within that nucleus, of course, are the Special Volunteers whose missions are detailed in the records for your sectors.

"We have gathered here for the purpose of reconciling all of our efforts toward the unveiling and the training of the Earth leaders, and to bring all of our separate plans in harmony with the whole. I am aware that all of you have labored long, and in the presence of great opposition, to fulfill your scheduling for this event. It is clear that all councils will not occur at one given moment, but within each sector it is hoped that all candidates will participate at one time. We have now agreed that there will be seven worldwide sectors or divisions by area, in which these gatherings will take place.

"In our meetings that follow, these seven sector Commanders will share with you their detailed plans and will receive your comments and counter suggestions concerning them. We ask of you only that in your attention upon these seven leaders, you will take back with you into your varied areas of responsibilities, the vibration of concern and urgency that you feel in our midst today.

"These Gatherings are the apex of the wedge in the salvation of a planet. These Elect ones will be our hands and feet and our voices for the time that remains between now and the coming removal of the Lighted Ones from the planet. We have attempted to discern the times in Earth calculations of time, when events will bring on these contingencies. However, it is impossible at this moment to give you or anyone else any distinct date or time reference. The date of each individual council will be determined here today, but the span of time before the first evacuation cannot be determined. Therefore, we must maintain and continue in our total readiness at all times, for the call may reach us at any moment.

"Our friends of the Jupiter Command are keeping us posted within seconds of Earth time, on every smallest detail of events *BEFORE THEY HAPPEN!* They are doing an excellent work in monitoring the secret government councils of the world nations. They not only register all of the proposed plans, but evaluate each leader within his emotional and rational being to determine his probable response to any given set of circumstances. So far, they have been one-hundred percent correct in this type of analysis, making it an indispensable source of recurrence for the entire program. It allows us to be just a little ahead of mankind in their own access to reports of world events.

"Therefore, I share with you the excitement of this moment in getting 'on with it,' so to speak, and bringing all of our preparations and plans into focus and action. As spokesman for the Saturnian Council of this Solar System, I welcome you to these policy decisions and will be enjoying meeting with as many of you as possible at this conclave. My gratitude is extended to our gracious hosts, Commander Anton, of Cook Mountain; and Captain Avalon, of this great communications center; and to our Chairman, Commander Ashtar. Ladies and gentlemen, I thank you."

* * *

(Avalon once again: "Thank you, Tuella. Following Mon-

ka's sweep of applause, a lesser speaker is directing the participants to the smaller meeting locations. We will return at 10:00
to check on events at that time. Avalon closing the contact.")

At 10:00, Avalon reported that there had been a scurry of
activity as assignments for different committee meetings were
given. There was a lounging break for fellowship and refresh-
ments which, he assured me, did not include coffee and dough-
nuts! This was to be the last session until we returned at 2:00
that afternoon, when Beloved Jesus-Sananda would be speaking.

Korton Speaks at the Great Council

A Commander from the Veldor sector introduced Korton,
and he gave this message:

"Highly respected and honorable Lords and Ladies of
many worlds, many galaxies and faraway places, it is my privilege to be with you and to bring you some thoughts of our
group concerning the purposes for which we have gathered.

"During these summer months on Earth, we have all been
very active organizing ourselves for these coming special Gatherings. Our work will soon be concluded and these seven
Councils with our Earth Leaders can begin. Our many preparations have taken much time, and details have been going on
at a feverish pace.

"Basically, the communication devices we have proposed
are to be fairly identical in all seven divisions. They need not be
the same in appearance, but in function they must be the same.
As the needs were presented to each group quite some time
ago, it has been ingenious the diversity of designs that have
been brought forth, yet all do indeed coordinate with all others
in the functions performed and the vital needs fulfilled. There
will be an identifying crystal of certain color for each, which
immediately indicates the group to which that person is
assigned, as well as the Sector Commander. This central stone
will also be the crystal that is in attunement with the body
vibrations of the one who wears it and who is in direct contact

with his Commander craft. The device will also have a factor incorporated into its design which will serve as a levitating or traveling device for any emergency, as well as another built-in deposit of crystalline energy functioning as the means of producing invisibility as needed in times of danger. Of all the equipment with which we will arm our Earthean Eagles, the greatest will be the unveiling of their memories and the revelation of their identities and missions to the planet Earth.

"We are also greatly pleased to at last be able to bring about a complete network of acquainting them all with one another so that they may know as we are known and can meet face to face with their coworkers in this plan. There will be a great love between them as they labor together and help one another.

"All of us who make up the Commands patrolling the Earth have longed to see this unity and coordinating action take place on physical levels. These great Gatherings will bring this to pass and Heaven and Earth will enjoy a unity of purpose unknown for millions of cycles. In daring to let our representatives be exposed to the Earth world, we have taken great care in planning how this would be done. By stationing those who are a part of our mission within the ranks of world media, we will be able to do this in a simultaneous break of the news releases, that will eliminate all opposition, and will at least give us an honest reporting of events. A few large interests will withhold the story, but will later get on the bandwagon as so many consistently begin to come forth. The lives of our representatives will be intensely protected while their testimony is being given and carrying on. Other representatives everywhere will join in their defense. It is this daring exposure of those who serve with us that will turn the hearts of the multitudes to consider the words of these few. Total recall will be permitted in their ranks and all will return with a fully operating spiritual opening of their abilities to handle every spiritual need which confronts them. All will become spokesmen for the Commands

PROJECT: WORLD EVACUATION

and teachers of truth. At best, their testimony will be brief, lasting only until the evacuations begin, but vital in their intensity and impact.

"This is the program, ladies and gentlemen, with which the world will be turned. This is also the method with which evacuation will be carried on from the Earth level. All of these self-sacrificing leaders will remain until the *last moment* for directing others, teaching others, and assisting in the creation of an atmosphere free of fear around those clusters of humanity preparing for their rescue. It is this Special Legion who will be answering questions, teaching the people, and preparing their hearts for that which is to come. Without them, our mission could not proceed in its purpose, for the aura of fear and hostility toward us still prevails on a general scale.

"We will be working closely together in our committee meetings to coordinate these many details and prepare ourselves for action as soon as possible. There is not a moment of Earth time to be wasted in this preparation. The sound of war comes ever closer, and the planet within prepares its response! We must make haste in our final proposals and go forth from this great conclave with all final decisions agreed upon. We must have unity in the midst and the willingness to surrender our desired suggestions for the benefit of the whole and completion of our work here.

"Again, I thank you for this opportunity to speak with all of you and to be a part of this great council for so important a mission. Thank you, my brothers and sisters, on whom the Light of our Radiant One ever shines! I thank you."

* * *

As requested, I returned to the typewriter a little before 2:00 p.m., and was then given the privilege of hearing The Great Beloved Commander in Chief, Jesus the Christ, and recording His message for this volume.

44

Beloved JESUS-SANANDA
Addresses The Great Council

"Courageous, loyal and devoted Lords and Ladies of this and many great galaxies, you have given me a very pleasant chore this afternoon, in speaking and meeting with all of our dedicated Leaders and Directors of our great Intergalactic program for Peace. I am the honored one in beholding your beautiful countenances and responding to the love that flows through each one of your beings and outward toward Me.

"I have come to join with all of you in this final preparation for that great event which we have planned together for so long. It is a great moment for my own heart, as it is for yours. We have not only labored in the planning for the event, we have likewise labored in the effort to prevent its necessity. Now we must secure our decisions and go forward with our Plan.

"In the beginning of our active programming we will have the assistance of the entire Angel Kingdom, under the supervision of Michael and His Legions. El Morya will exercise his administration of the Blue Flame of protection and build a wall of Blue Fire around each chela who is destined to be taken into your midst and to be returned again for the final stages of their service to humanity. Each one, I am assured, will be surrounded in the circle Blue Flame from the first divine ray of manifestation, and Michael's Angels will be bodyguards to them all. All of this attention, plus your own beams upon them directly from your craft, should well protect them and their mission from all harm and interference.

"We have brought all of you together in this conference for a feeling of encouragement as well as for practical reasons. Let us join in Love to one another as we realize that the long battle soon will end, that our efforts for the planet Earth shall soon see fruition and the joyful reunion of all of us with our brothers and sisters in service there.

"We have great things and great surprises in store for them, and words cannot describe the joy with which we antici-

45

pate this great reunion. We must realize and understand that both the leadership meetings and the evacuation stages may be a great shock to some of them. Their human reactions may be unprepared for these events. It is for this reason that a book is now being prepared through the coordinated efforts of Kuthumi and the Ashtar Command, in which most of these details will be revealed to all the souls of Light. I have requested that this very conclave be included in its contents. We have had to proceed with great caution in revealing our strategy and plans for this new touch with mankind. We have had to consider his binding theological prejudices, his apathy, his indifference, his general close-mindedness in most of these things, but most of all, his outright hostility to those whom the Father has sent to reason with him. Because of this militancy, our progress for the world plan has been delayed for twenty-five years. Many have wearied that it would ever come to pass, not only of your group, but our Earth contactees as well.

"We are trusting that the witness of these Special Leaders and their campaign outlining the Divine Program of rescue by those whom the Father will send to them, will in that dark hour of Earth's evacuation, proceed with a minimum of interference from man.

"I send a special dispensation of annointing for this task upon all of these whom you will take into your midst. They shall carry within their inner being great power and perseverance in this ongoing battle for the minds of men. They shall not be left unequipped without the proper spiritual weapons with which to carry forward this encounter. All shall be filled with spiritual power and annointed to meet every need from the overflow of their inward blessings.

"They will have constant attunement with those of you who guard them and guide their ministries. The mystical objects you have prepared for them represent a great contribution for their behalf, and this will secure for them all of the remaining protection that is necessary. When the days of evacuation are upon us, these will be the ones to whom you will turn for the help that is needed upon Terra. Those few moments of feverish action will bring about the gathering of the wheat into My barn for the eternal harvest.

"I convey to you, ladies and gentlemen, the total gratitude of the Celestial Government of this Solar System for your long participation in the Divine Plan for planet Earth. Yours is the supreme example of that kind of life that has been held out to mankind through many eons of time. As you fellowship with them, they will see and absorb the Love that abounds within you and will be drawn to your governing philosophies of freedom and respect for the divine image within all of the Father's creation. My blessings radiate to each one of you and overshadow you with the emanations of my own Light as you have so beautifully earned the 'well done' of Our Father. Friends of the highest purity and worthiness, I thank you."

Thus spoke Our Lord Jesus, or, as He is known to them, Beloved Great Commander Sananda—the Radiant One—to all of these great Ones in attendance at this vital Tribunal.

The Hosts of Heaven
Sponsor a Feast!

Undoubtedly most of you, just as I, have wondered about many of the "onboard" details of these conferences.

Raymond Fowler tells us, "From the experience I have had on space ships, I can tell you briefly that their crews utilize the higher cosmic frequencies to run their power plants and generate the forcefield which they put about them in a 360° sphere in which they can hover or travel at fantastic speeds in any direction in all types of atmospheres. Also, there is an energy field within the ships. These ships can lower their frequencies or accelerate them, according to the direction they wish to go to fulfill their missions."

Ashtar has plainly said, "You will be hosted by us, fed, and housed comfortably in a great mother ship." On another occasion, Andromeda Rex answered my question about the cuisine: "It will be as nearly normal to your accustomed foods as we can arrange it. It will include some drinks and foods that are new to you, but we are attempting a cuisine that will be favorable to all, with personal choices where needed."

Earlier, Captain Avalon had surprised me with his comment: "You will be impressed with our culinary skills."

To get into more important matters, the remainder of the beautiful message from Andromeda Rex, through messenger Lucy Colson, given especially for this book, continues:

"At the Gathering, there will be a welcoming reception,

with the mingling of Beings from all worlds. A truly exciting time, for we introduce the Eartheans to their Galaxy and Universe! The first time in thousands of years that Earth has participated on the scale which she will now. We are grateful that at long last she comes back into the fold. The purpose of the Gathering will be fully explained at that time, with a full discussion of the potential crisis to the planet and its inhabitants; the decisions reached by the Planetary Hierarchy; and the role that you Earth Beings will now play in restoring life to the planet. Assignments of Commanders will be made, and then each Commander will meet with the group under him/her to firm up decisions and make plans.

"Since you Earthly Light Commanders will have a closer and even a bodily contact with us over the next few years, or whenever evacuation must be executed (it is absolutely dependent upon mankind's Free Will), at this very moment we are preparing for each one of you a pendant. This is no ordinary pendant, but one similar to those worn in Atlantis by those working in the strong electromagnetic fields around the crystals. In the center of the pendant is a small body crystal which we are attuning to the vibrational frequencies of each Commander. Preparation of the crystals is going on at *a feverish pace* aboard the host Command ship.

"As each person is welcomed aboard, he or she will have a pendant slipped around the neck, never to be removed again in bodily form. Upon the body's death, should that happen, the pendant will immediately dissolve. The body crystal attuned to each one's vibrational pattern will help each to tolerate changes in frequencies on the Earth plane as well as when aboard the Command ships. Ships, yes. Each will receive a special assignment and report to that specific Mother Ship involved with a particular of Command. We need use a word of caution here, that not all be revealed at this stage.

"Communication will also be greatly enhanced through mental telepathy, as by wearing the body crystal, one's vibrations will be stepped up and a more synchronous match can be established between the realms. A matter of vibration is all that defines dimensions. We cannot give any more information at this time without divulging classified information to the public. Not everyone who will read your forthcoming book, Tuella, will be of the Light. Therefore, we are not permitted to go any further, just as you will not be permitted to give out time, dates and whatnot.

"To reiterate. First, there will be the Gathering of the Eagles. This Gathering will consist of many of the Lord's Hosts, two or more contingencies from a far galaxy who will arrive in the Earth's atmosphere in time for their participation. Expertly trained for planetary evacuation in time of dire need, these brave Souls of Light have volunteered to assist us as we now reach the crisis point in Earth's destination.

"After the meeting and blending of those who come from the Planet Earth itself, a triune Council will be formed—The Ascended Master/Angelic Realm, the Universal, and the Earth—all blended together as one with one common bond, the survival of man, that he may evolve into MAN. HuMan (Heavenly, Universal, Man).

"After that Conclave, then the real Gathering of the Light Commanders takes place after that event, the real work commences as all Heaven and Light upon the Earth strive to bring the planet Earth into its proper alignment with the Christ potential. *The advent of the Christ Light [not a PERSON] between December 15 and December 30 will create great turmoil.* Most inhabitants of Earth cannot endure the vibrations as they are, let alone what they will become. You will have much work to do by then. Evacuation plans should be on schedule, but we need everyone's help to make this possible. I thank you. I am Andromeda Rex."

* * *

As we present the messages coming to several others

50

within this revelation on the various topics covered, it is hoped that the children of Light will realize this is not something coming to just one source, but that the same trend of information is coming to us now through many different space channels, like the rush of a mighty river. I have spoken with too many to quote all of them here, but as I present the same questions for reasons of confirmation, the answers all correlate in a remarkable way.

After the announcement to begin the book in Utah, and the nature of the earlier dictations, while there I joined with messenger Eve Carney, to undertake some in-depth research on the subject. This was several weeks before Andromeda's discourse with Lucy was received, and included in our research was my first inkling of the color-coded concept in the evacuation. We learned that different colored ships will pick up individuals with the different colored auras, or energy fields. Blue-coded ships will pick up blue aura persons, etc. For example, one ship is responsible for lifting all medical personnel, volunteers, with the ship corresponding to the nature of the classification of the workers. For example, a yellow ship under the auspices of the ray of wisdom and knowledge will pick up educators, writers and intelligent persona; pink ships will pick up persons whose calling is to love emanations and mother vibrations and the young children, for whom there has been total preparation on board. The purpose for giving the crystal in color matching the designated ships is to enable that ship to maintain contact with those it has had on board for briefing time.

Almost a year before, I had been informed that at the Commander briefings we would return with "something to wear and something to carry." In researching that statement, we learned the things persons will bring back with them had different colored stones. Some had necklaces; some, brooches; rings; but all set with crystal stones; even something to wear in their hair, just as long as these crystals were upon their form. Apparently the craft would use these devices to zero in on them, as energy devices.

Concerning "something to carry," Eve saw some persons given a "little box comparable in size to the little cereal boxes" which contained what appeared to her to be little scrolls. Some of the key personnel are given these. Some are even given handkerchiefs that are monogrammed in the corner with the scroll. What they were given was evidently determined by the particular Mother Ship that housed them for the council. Eve said, "The people will be categorized, so to speak, and leaders in each category will be chosen, and they are the ones who will be given these small gold parchment scrolls which are contained in the small boxes."

A few weeks later, when I was privileged to report the addresses given at the final planning Council for the Gatherings, and I heard Korton alluding to the "diversity of designs" of these devices that had been submitted from the several sectors, yet "coordinate with all others in functions performed," I understood why there has been some discrepancy in description of these devices from various sources. If a spiritual messenger is from one sector, they may see the design that one will use, while a messenger from another sector may see an object different in appearance. Korton did also confirm that "there will be an identifying crystal of certain color for each which immediately indicates the group to which that person is assigned, as well as the sector Commander." All are agreed on this fact of the body crystal and its function.

We also tuned in to some very interesting information regarding the missions of a few very elderly women, who have donated their lifetime simply toward building up the Light within them. These will be picked up for the Gatherings and be given the handkerchiefs within the different groups, which are monogrammed in the corner accordingly. The special assignment of these elderly ladies has been just to stay alive (some are in nursing establishments and will only be taken out of body so as not to be missed) and hold the Light and prayer for the volunteers of their specific group. Thus each group will have its Leader, its Love person, its teacher, writer, reporter, healers, scientists, and so forth. These elderly channels of Light will wear their handkerchiefs to be visible to the people of their group on the spacecraft. They will be given so much energy that wherever the others of her group are, in their night sleep they will be able to "plug into" this Love Person for their energy needs. This will be their sole contribution to their overall program.

* * *

At one time in the past, I had asked Ashtar to discuss the human forcefield, and he replied:

"The magnetics of the human aura are a forcefield. The heart is the central atom around which neutrons, cells and electrons gravitate. Blood goes out from the heart, makes its circle and returns again, enabling the physical form to give off energy in framework as force. Force continues in an ovoid shape which you call the auric field, but it is more than that. This force represents a magnetism to other magnetic force of the frequency. So like attracts like, it is said. Now, when the field is of high frequency, color disappears into white Light. When the human orbit or magnetic field is white Light, we then say that one has transmuted the physical form of density to a Light body. This Light body or forcefield is that which makes contact and exposure to our magnetic field possible. You would suffer no discomfort in our presence. The forcefield of Light pulls and is pulled ever higher. Your constant exposure to our frequencies greatly infuses your own with higher frequencies."

While preparing this text, he said that, "while within our great Mother Ship of my own Command fleet and hosted by our staff, you will be subjected to many different kinds of experiences designed to correlate your physical with your spiritual attainment. The physical form will take on great beauty and an essence of Light will radiate to those with eyes to see. The entire being will become changed into that which you once were, yet when you return those who know you not will simply continue to see that outward appearance. But spiritually aware persons will see the difference in the eyes, the magnetism and the glow of the person, and the radiance of the countenance."

I asked if this change would take place within all who attended?

"Yes, but with some who have not started this process at all, the workings will only have begun, so the immediate change will not be so noticeable as with those in whom the process began some time ago. Those who are just beginning will sense youthful energy so that they feel exhilarated; with others, it will be completed. Minds also will be quickened by the rays in which you will sit, and the emotional body will be brought under total control and instructions and directives given. Youthfulness of action and appearance accompanies the presence of the Light body. Generally speaking, those who know not your inner qualities will see your appearance the same, yet there will be that different quality about you some-how. They will say you're 'looking good,' and that sort of thing. But to those spiritually aware of your Light, you will appear much younger, youthful of energy and movement. The presence of Light itself within the physical form tends to reju-venate and reactivate all the cells of the body; thus, no illness can enter this teeming life action, and the energy that enters find no impediments to its flow. Therefore, the change into the Light body brings these outward changes as a result of the inner workings of the Light. It is a natural as well as scientific action, actually. In the completion of this action one has desire for a lesser quantity of food and tends toward drinking of more liquids."

I wondered how the transposition to the Light body would affect concentration, telepathy and clairvoyance? Andromeda Rex was answering questions at this time: "This will differ with some according to their needs and to their mis-sion. All do not need all of these abilities; however, most do.

Where necessary, some will have a full opening of the chakras take place, under our surveillance while you are with us. This action can be speeded up as long as you are under careful examination. It would be harmful to some in the present to open them so suddenly. Others will be quickened in the area of their need, for that which they are commissioned to accomplish. But All will have telepathic abilities induced, for this is most necessary that you be able to communicate with one another efficiently and with us at all times."

Another problem that needed clarification in my own thinking was the concept of compressed time. In the research with Eve Carney, we learned much about the difference in time in the different dimensions. Once beyond the atmosphere of the Earth, there is no time as we understand it. Weeks there can be as moments here, depending on the longitude and latitude of area from which departure is made.

For these secret Gatherings, some will be merely taken out of body, and seem to be away only a "twinkling of an eye," when the time gone will be almost unnoticeable, and only be absent three to five minutes. Different ones will be gone different periods of time. Some will be taken in the physical form and will actually be physically absent for two to three weeks Earth time. It seems that a day of Earth time can be as two weeks with them. While some will indeed be absent up to nearly 21 days, others will only be away three to four days. Eve explained: "They are saying 'twinkling of an eye,' and I'm feeling three to five minutes. A husband could walk outside to pull a few weeds and come back in and his wife will have been gone two to three weeks, and to him, she may have seemed to have gone elsewhere in the home for three to five minutes or so. Some of those who go will be away much longer than others. The highest ranking leaders of the project will be gone longer than the others, much longer."

These answers greatly assisted in reconciling some of the seemingly inconsistent details that had been received. Nevertheless, many really stupid questions chased one another through my inquisitive mind. For example, many humans prefer to sleep in the nude, and if they are taken off into other worlds at that time, what are they wearing? (I *said* they were stupid!) One afternoon when Kuthumi was on the Cosmic Telephone, I asked him (he tolerates me quite well). He offered these details:

"The spiritual essence of one who sleeps is automatically woven a covering by those who serve as escorts, for one never travels or journeys into other worlds alone! By thought, escorts create a garment of white to be worn at all times out of body wherever one goes. There are times when the occasion calls for a greater finery, and it is provided—including your crown."

Many months previous to this particular research, I had been told that the participants of these Secret Councils would be permitted to bring cameras and tape recorders for purposes of returning with more exclusive evidence. I had problems trying to understand how a person out of body could carry with him camera and recording supplies as instructed, and return with them as well. Dear Kuthumi obliged again:

"Another interesting question! The items that will be brought back are to be dematerialized and then materialized again in your dimension when that one awakens. This is an easy thing for us (!) and our brothers. As for the things to have been taken, the same process would be reversed, but the participant would be in an etheric body."

Many years ago at my home deep in the woods of southern Pennsylvania, my two daughters and I had been in a meditative moment together, when three Space Brothers appeared in the front yard. They preferred to remain outside when invited in, because of their height and my normal sized doors and ceilings. We were asked if we would enjoy visiting their ship, and we responded with a joyous affirmative. The appointment was made for the following evening at 8:00, and we were instructed to relax in a reclining position on the floor for meditation and an escort would come for us. We thanked our visitors and rushed outside. My daughters were able to see the ship up above, for they both have the gift of sight.

The following evening we relaxed as instructed, and set out upon our three separate meditation experiences. I left my body and rested my hands upon the forearms of my two escorts, and experienced the tremendous motion as we ascended at incredible speed upward to the waiting ship. I was immediately standing in the great map and control room looking at Athena, with tears streaming down my face. She also wept, and we embraced. Athena (a lady Commander) began showing me the various maps. I sensed that one daughter had gone down a long corridor, though I hadn't seen her, but knew she was elsewhere on the ship. We did walk by a great glass wall through which I could see my other daughter reclining on a medical examination the table, and someone with her. This was the extent of my recall—very very brief and fragmentary.

In just a few minutes—not more than fifteen—all three of us were "back" to this consciousness and we began comparing our recalls. The one daughter *had* been down a long corridor which was lined with garment lockers. She had opened one, and they were filled with golden jumpsuits. She pulled one out, and it had her name embossed on it across the left chest area. She was grounded in shock, and put it back.

She also had seen her sister on a medical table. The other daughter recalled only that she was "getting some kind of a treatment." She knew it was good, and the attendant was her spiritual lady doctor, a member of her guidance group. That was all that any of us could recall. At least the invitation had been kept, and we were satisfied enough with the excursion.

Nine years later, when the research into this compressed time concept was unfolding at Utah this summer, I pounced in excitedly with my question: "Well, then, would you please tell me how long my daughters and I were on that Mother Ship during our fifteen minutes of meditation"? The answer came fast and startling: *"EIGHT HOURS!"* Some explanation was forth-coming. First of all, we were being climatized, acclimated on inner levels for future on-board experiences. We had been per-mitted just enough fragments of recall to be consistent with each other's accounts and memories of having seen each other in instances that were correct. Further, the "treatment" being administered to the daughter on the medical table was a process administered for the opening of a chakra. I had only been able to recall being in the control room looking at maps with Athena. Actually I had been shown the large scanning screens with flashes of scenes from lesser ships over other countries and seas. I had observed the groups in the mountains and their works. It had been a bit like a general briefing on communications.

I asked, and was informed, that no implants had been placed in any of us. It was further explained, interestingly enough, that implants are never used by the extraterrestrials who serve the Light except within those who are not of our evolution. For those on special service *direct from the ships*, not born of Earth woman, but materialized on Earth as special envoys on special missions, out of necessity, do have implants within them for purposes of survival in our atmosphere and close contact with their Command. But the Legions of Light *NEVER* place implants within humanity without their knowl-edge or consent, for this would violate Universal Law.

Kuthumi explained: "The dark souls often become wired during their vulnerable periods because of wrong living—for example, while intoxicated or on drugs. This means they are totally out of control of their vehicles and mind, and have become, unknowingly, practically human robots. Children of the Light cannot be placed in this situation because they have placed their will in Higher Hands for safekeeping, by placing God's will first in all the details of their lives."

The other daughter, who had seen the golden jumpsuit uniform bearing her name, was being activated at that time, we were told. They had stimulated her psychic centers. We were told that my daughters have since then been upon the ships frequently. One of them had been with them once for a very long time while her body slept. I was told that my own excursions while out of body have mainly involved participation within the mountain-base installations. I have recounted this entire incident specifically that those who read this account will realize that when you return to wakefulness or from meditation, with some small fragment of recall of a ship's surroundings or an extraterrestrial's conversation, or some other heavenly scene, it is highly likely that you have actually not only been there, but have been there for an extended period of time.

That which we do not or are not permitted to recall is, nevertheless, programmed into our inner being to be triggered at a later date when needed. Total recall will flash its intrusion into your human consciousness when events warrant this action.

To conclude our thoughts on compressed time, I quote another portion of the message received by Lucy Colson from Andromeda Rex for inclusion in this text:

"Depending on the openings into your dimension at the time of your Gathering, you will either be beamed aboard physically, or it will of necessity be an out-of-body experience. In either event, time can be compressed for those who must not leave their areas for more than one night in the physical body, so what would normally be a two-week meeting would be an eight-hour expanse of Earth time for that person. *Each will return consciously aware of their orders and all aspects of the meetings.*"

Andromeda Rex continues, "To return to the above statement about the openings into third dimension, with all of the acute electromagnetic activity from the planetary events in your heavens, dimensional warping is taking place. Certain doors which are normally open paths between realms are closing temporarily during certain planetary configurations—most important to note is the Jupiter/Saturn conjunctions. When Mars is heavily aspected, we also find the narrowing of the dimensional passageways. This is not a reference to the ley lines, but a passageway between them."

This new concept of dimensional warping certainly gears the mind toward further investigation, but I did not have the time at this writing to pursue the matter.

* * *

An interesting discourse concerning further "on-board" matters was passed along by Captain Avalon, of the Floridian Mountains Communication Center,during one of our relaxed conversations:

"The trees on our ship (imagine...trees!) are artificially cared for, but they are *real* trees. We also have many grassed areas. The walkways are bordered by grassed areas. You will have a small apartment with a built-in bed about 4 feet wide with storage compartments around it. There is a small shower and sink and facilities. In the remaining space there are two chairs for lounging, and a small table, screens and speakers for communication and entertainment. There are a few shelves and a mirror. The bed is a medium-firm texture with a thin coverlet. The floor covering is sanitary, feels and looks like cloth, but it isn't. We have indirect lighting with intensifying switches for the degree of brightness as desired. You will be called softly at awakening time or from daytime rest periods, which are incorporated into the schedule, as well as social relaxation periods. You may bring your toilet articles and care for yourself just as you would at home." More than a year ago Athena had confided that on her Mother Ship there was a small living area with my name on the door. I had mostly rejected the information at the time, being unable to compute it into my understanding of the moment. But since these new things have come along, I pulled her statement forth from my memory bank for reconsideration. In fact, I have dared to toy with the idea of "why not just leave my possessions in the drawers, etc., since I'll be back at the end of the evacuation!" What a home-away-from-home!

Rather, perhaps the reverse is true. Captain Avalon interrupted my mental meandering to confirm: "These are the same quarters you will be taken to in the later evacuation action."

In true womanlike reaction, I was also curious about what to wear, what to include in the little suitcase. I was told that the atmosphere on board would be near a comfortable 65° to 70°, and that there would be no perspiration. Suits and light jackets would be appropriate.

"You may dress in your typical casual wear, planning perhaps for one formal attire for dinner. You will all receive a robe-type garment to be worn for certain occasions. You will have social periods, and rest periods. The days will be programmed similar to any of your Earth conventions, with scheduled times for the various activities. You are encouraged to include your tape recorder and notebook and pen and your camera. All of these will be permitted at different times, though not all of the time. The weekends will include banquets which will surprise you. Our culinary skills are quite good!"

There remained only one further matter concerning life on board their craft on which I sought information. I asked if there would be medical treatments or physical examinations given while on board. Andromeda Rex was in contact at the time:

* * *

"Yes. All who enter must undergo a physical examination to determine the exact status of the physical form. This will be for the purpose of personal adjustment when entering into the cubicle in which the Light Body is rejuvenated. Just as many of your own medical profession would require an examination before diagnosis and procedures. Any medical treatment that is necessary will be immediately disposed of by our electronic equipment and technology. Then we will proceed to the body change into Light Force. *None will return with less than a perfect body.* It is ordained as one of the necessities of service of this nature. There will be built-in energy responses which will guarantee energy drive at all times, with alertness and above-average abilities in quick mental response and telepathic qualities. Vision will be strengthened and made keen beyond the usual nature of human vision. This is a most-needed tool. We intend to equip our representatives with all of the best in every way possible. We also intend to flow to all of you all that is needed in the way of capital for carrying out what must be done. None shall know want or deprivation, but all shall live in what is termed a comfortable manner according to their choice. As they desire, they shall have, in keeping with a dedicated motivation for service."

Without my having asked, the following details were volunteered:

"Newer followers of our Light will be allowed many question and answer periods, and many so-called 'rap-sessions' will be part of the program. Many who come will have earned the right to be with us by virtue of commitment and having passed the qualifying tests, yet they may not be completely learned in the program and purpose of the Confederation. ALL must be thoroughly grounded in this before departure."

I was prompted to ask, "Will we know the identity and whereabouts of only those in our own Council, or perhaps, the entire Command Ground Force?"

Answer: "Certain of you will have access to the knowledge of the entire ground force of this new offensive (not those of former ones) while others will be made aware of the full information pertaining to those with whom they will be associated because of the nature of their mission. The amount of information to be retained will be dispensed on a 'need to know' basis. Higher ranking individuals will have access to more detailed information than others."

I was further advised that certain participants especially well documented as extrovert in manner and social exchange, would be called upon to serve as co-hosts in producing a relaxed atmosphere for all of these strangers to get to know one another. Some of these chosen co-hosts may be lifted a day or two in advance of the others, to assist the Brothers in greeting the guests. These would be toured through quarters and areas for familiarizing them with the facilities. This simple aforehand maneuver will greatly assist the Brothers in settling the great number of guests. It will, it is said, greatly cushion the expectancy of some, to be met by an Earth person along with the Brothers, and contribute to ease of mind. They have said:

"We must be very certain that those we have gathered together are equal in thought, word and deed, and of one mind. Therefore, we will require a certain period of orientation at the beginning which is designed to expose all of you to one another and which will break down any rigidness or standoffishness within our gatherings. We must have openness and free interchange of personal feelings and adaptation. Even though certain souls are exceedingly enthusiastic for our cause, and beautifully dedicated to it, they may not necessarily be without personality flaws and social awkwardness. Our co-hosts will be of great assistance to us in opening these withdrawn types of participants.

"After this initial visit, which, as you know, is primarily for evidential purposes, you will have many other visits with us, but none will be so important as this one."

Concerning the personnel of these Gatherings, they had this to say:

"There will be legal counselors, medical personnel, technical scientists, public relations persons, persons in the media, persons of great religious convictions, experienced educational majors, political scientists, and law enforcement persons. The arts will be greatly represented and the creative media as well. There will be those who excel in the theatrical fields and entertainment world also, who will win many by their story. There will be represented every kind of ability and leadership, along with a spiritual willingness to cooperate and work as a team toward one goal. This will be stressed greatly, as it is most necessary.

"Any who attempt to use these contacts for personal gain or selfish purposes will immediately be dropped from the Forces. There will be other writers and two other publishers also active in the program."

Kuthumi has remarked, "The bringing in of these Earth volunteers to a state of fellowship under these extraordinary circumstances will vitalize all of you to such an intense state of energy and enthusiasm that you will never forget it, never get over it, never lose the vision for it until all things are come to pass! This will be the firing of your personal momentum in a most spectacular way and will bring into all of you, the inner level awakening you need. No one will leave these briefings without all chakras attended to, all physical problems removed, and all obstacles removed from the pathway of your mission. You will be equipped with every kind of gadgetry assistance, as well as spiritual weapons for all challenges to your ministry."

Returning to the Battle

"This is Ashtar. I come as an emissary of our Beloved and Radiant One. I am a Light Being who speaks to you in His Name, and I represent the Commands of this hemisphere." With all of this preliminary protocol dispensed with, Ashtar continued:

"We are in intense preparations for these Councils. Our desire is to meet with all of you personally on a face-to-face basis. This will anchor within you an experience that will carry you through anything that will follow. These dedicated ones will enter this experience not only for their own blessing and personal needs for their work, but primarily for a witness to the world. This is the testimony we would have them give to the world, the account of their face-to-face encounter with the Commanders of the Extraterrestrial Forces of the Space Confederation.

"You shall be taken into that place where our etheric cities are in waiting. Now is the time when the world must know, and believe, and accept these things. This book you are preparing now could very well forestall all atomic war and all geological destruction if the hearts of men would receive our words.

"You see, the old revelations no longer grasp the attention of the people. There must be an injection of new material to awaken the urgency within mankind to think seriously at this crucial time of Earth's evolution. We are constantly in need of new testimonies, new recorded experiences, as souls tend to ignore the old and the past. We must have new voices to keep

65

the vision before the present generation.

"We declare to you, our messenger, that physical evidences will be given our representatives, which will not only sustain them, but which they will bring back to the world for the expansion of Light and Understanding to men of Earth."

* * *

"I am Andromeda Rex, of the Intergalactic Council of the Space Confederation, and your speaker for this hour. All of you will strengthen the testimony of each other. They cannot call it conspiracy if the evidential material is in all of your hands. For were they to remove it from you, it will appear elsewhere. And so, in this manner we protect our work and our witnesses. Many books will come forth from the Gatherings and a fresh input of information and enthusiasm. We realize, along with you, that the input of other generations has cooled and grown too accustomed by most. It no longer electrifies in the manner that is needed. Therefore, we propose to jolt new fire and interest into our program by these representatives who will sojourn with us for this brief exposure to witness to the reality of our existence and purpose. This new program will be all that is needed to carry the momentum into and throughout the cleansing period and the inauguration of the New Age on Earth. All of you who come will be the Initiators of that New Age program.

"We send our love and deepest gratitude for all of the assistance rendered to us, without which, we could not accomplish the mission of Hope and Light to planet Earth."

Sir, you have stated that upon returning, we are to become open witnesses to the fact of our representation of your Commands above. Is there not some sort of illegality to be reckoned with in being the representative of an alien government?

Answer: "That is a good question, Tuella. Let's discuss the matter. It is true in a certain sense that as an alien from another Earth government this would apply. And of course, considering the hostility of your Earth governments, this would probably also apply in the present. However, I wish to point out to all of you involved that you do not represent an alien helpless government. You will be backed by all of our enabling intervention in any problem that might arise. So often your own CIA personnel are required to enter into missions in which they can do no calling upon those who have sent them. They cannot in any way reveal their identity or their source of authority. In the case of our representatives, such is not the case. On the contrary, you will have full and open access to all of our abilities to protect you, to work with you in confusing those who would harm you, and convincing them of the truth of your ambassadorship. For remember, this is our only purpose, to get them to listen attentively to the messages being sent to them.

"If this same activity is happening in many countries all over the globe simultaneously, there will be much serious thought given to the matter. Further, there will be a protesting uprising against those in office who might seek in any way to do harm to those whom God has sent. This is not the day of the Sanhedrin and Pilate's court; this is your world, in which people *can* make themselves heard if they choose to do so.

"Your people have read of these things and received and believed the words and the witness of our Commanders and their visit in our midst. They will hasten to stand up and be heard, and that from many high places. Basically that which you will all say and do stems from your personal religious experience and convictions, and under your Constitution, you do have that right to act upon your personal religious principles.

"However, if the powers that be indeed wanted to become belligerent and unduly ugly, then they could stress obscure technicalities as grounds for incarceration. But a few visits and occurrences from us would soon end all such. And if necessary, we would simply remove or transport our faithful who were so treated.

67

"Have no fear of any of these earthly reverberations, for we will have all things in hand. This will be easier to believe and understand once you have seen our equipment in operation with your own eyes. Then fear will be impossible within you."

* * *

I have been given to understand that the returning will be to exactly the spot from which lift-off occurred.

Further, whether or not full consciousness is retained during this removal and return with full recall, will be an individual matter and depend upon the person and the assignment. Full recall is not permitted to all because in that manner the Commands would lose control of their own program. By limiting it to only those who can handle it, they remain in control of their own program. Some will have recall triggered through the system at a certain time, because egos and personalities are involved. To prevent these from interfering with the plan, their recall will have to be triggered later. That is partly where the body crystals play a part.

* * *

We have these words from Commander Jycondria, Assistant to Ashtar, received by spiritual messenger Lyara, of Golden Rays Center, Phoenix:

"The Eagles, 'missionaries from space,' who are to receive these messages, will be surprised at both the variety and importance of their final assignments. The leaders of this final work will emerge from those of you who have quietly prepared in this lifetime for the fulfillment of visions and destinies they have known they are working for. Each wave of vibrational tuning up that has been accomplished on this planet has brought forth spiritual leaders who effected and supported these spiritual advancements through writings, teachings, music, arts, drama, inventions, science, etc. Like a surfer emerging on the crest their voice and influence has been spiritually uplifting to humanity. Now, as this fall progresses, will come forward the last wave cresting as it sweeps o'er the planet, with the leaders assigned to leadership in organizing and participating in the successful evacuation.

"Some must deflect the energies of the darkened ones who throw their darts of destruction, attempting to interfere with this work. Guard well against psychic, etheric and psychological attacks, for subtly working their destructive bends through these vehicles can be more deadly than releasing the atom bomb. Work confidently and wisely in the Light, knowing full well the power of God. Fear not any power as being apart from God, for what you fear, you will be subject to."

As we approach the conclusion of the message directed to the Intergalactic Legion of Special Volunteers from the Ashtar Command, it seems a proper place to present Kuthumi's summary of it all:

"In my Office of World Teacher, which I share with the Beloved Jesus-Sananda, we have often spoken together concerning the great darkness that fills the minds of men. Our work is sometimes discouraging, as we seek to penetrate the thought world of souls on Earth with shafts of Divine Light. The intuitive spiritual portion of the mind is so often overpowered and overshadowed by the preponderance of the intellect and the thinking processes. Yet there is a flame within man that brings knowing as an instinctive function and spiritual in nature.

"As events unfold in the discussions within this manuscript, it is our hope that spiritual intuition within the souls of men will respond, rather than intellectual reaction and debate. There are, as one has said, 'reasons which reason cannot understand.' The progress of civilization has brought humanity to a place of crisis and dangers to come. Now must come that day of separation so often spoken of by those Teachers who have attempted to shed Light on Terra. Now the wheat is to be separated from the chaff and be gathered by the Father, and the

PROJECT: WORLD EVACUATION

chaff tied in bundles to be burned.

"Who can speak of these things without the presence of sadness within his heart? Certainly not I. Yet I must speak, for the very words carry with them the emanations of love and hope that is shed upon those who read wisely. Take thought with me, if you will, to the acceleration of time that has taken place these recent months. So many have stated that events spoken of herein are not to be until the century ends. But these have not considered the acceleration that has taken place.

"Because of the release of atomic power, because of the heaviness of planetary vibrations, because of the release of the energies of the seven eclipses and the alignments of the planets, these are not ordinary times. These are times that will speak the end of the old order and the beginning of the new. This is the day of the new beginning. This is the day of the new Earth, and it must be made ready for its mission.

"I speak on behalf of the entire Spiritual Hierarchy when I plead with you to realize that 'time is short,' and whatever thou wouldst do toward spiritual expansion had best be done quickly. The coming onslaught will bring with it the end of materialistic dreams and objectionable goals.

"The inner planetary expulsions will soon be felt and be seen in an outward manifestation upon the surface of the land. As these things come to pass, many voices will be raised, and many great works will be seen, such as have never been seen. These will be the works of these who have been lifted into our midst, from whom the veils have been removed, and whose chakras have been fully opened. Souls who see them and hear them will know that these annointed ones have truly been with us and returned with a witness and the evidence that cannot be denied. For a 'brief moment of time' their ministries will be blessed and protected, and they shall no longer be secluded away without freedom of service. They shall stand boldly in many places, witnessing to the experiences that came to them in higher realms, where they were given a full insight to the events that are just before the world.

"When they have been raised in your midst, listen to these voices! These are the chosen and Elect Leaders, placed upon the planet by orders of the Spiritual Hierarchy and through collaboration of our beloved brothers from other dimensions and other worlds. These witnesses will return to you with the unction of authority upon their words and their deeds, that will convince and prepare many for the evacuation that is to follow.

"Their words shall remove fear and heal unbelief and expose the reality of that great invisible army of the Legions of Light that surround you. Every moment of the day, they monitor thoughts, words and deeds, and planetary responses, conditions and affairs. But a time will come when they are no longer able to contain the planetary action destined to come to pass. When those hours are upon you, many of you shall be prepared in your hearts, by these who return to you to give you our message. They have come as Volunteers to serve the Earth in her hour of trial. They shall be the spokesmen on the physical octave for those who remain in the higher dimensions. You shall know them by their fruits and by the evidence which they bring with them.

"We give warning to the world that ye seek not to destroy them, for that is not possible, and such an intention will precipitate grave results in your own lives. This inner circle of incarnated ones will walk amongst you when we have returned them to you. You will be electrified by their words and the story they have to tell the world. Since the creation of time, there has never been a time such as this, when the chosen and Elect Volunteers to Earth shall be gathered together to receive their credentials and their authority and sent back to bring these things before humanity. Hear my words, O beloved ones; take heed that you touch not a hair of their heads, for they also are emissaries of the Golden Light from other worlds. I am Kuthumi, and I bring you my blessing, my Love to all of you. My Light shines upon each and every one of you who read these words and handle this book."

PART II

The Three Evacuations

Mission of Mercy

We who are of more value than many sparrows find much assurance and comfort from these words of beloved Kuthumi, given especially for this book:

"The Spiritual Hierarchy of the Solar System has concluded that man has reached that point in his spiritual awakening when a fuller revelation of the closing portion of the Divine Plan for Earth may be revealed to him.

"This light is not a new thing. Glimmers have appeared here and there through many at different points in time. Yet broadly speaking, it has not been a known thing either. Or perhaps it has appeared in distorted form. It has not been stressed or particularly emphasized by us until this generation. There are many present, even within the folds of New Age concepts, who will cry that these things must not be spoken of. Yet where will *they* be when the word is needed to comfort the hearts of millions, when the sky is darkened with spacecraft, come to lift them to safety?

"So we must have our nucleus of messengers with the stamina and the courage to dare to get the message to the people of Earth, that this hour *will* come, and that when it *does*, there will be help ready in the skies to care for them! We do not involve ourselves with the dogmas of Earth or crystallizations of the doctrines of men. If our alerting messages or warnings or any portion thereof seems to be at odds with accepted traditional interpretations of things, *then let tradition update its information by returning to direct contact with the Celestial*

73

Government of this Solar System.

"Souls of Divine Illumination will not be overcome with fear because of a foreknowledge of coming events, but will, rather, be filled with a joyous confidence in the Heavenly Father and take refuge in His shadow until these calamities be passed. This, then, is your refuge from the storm, your shadow from the heat.

"With these revelations we share with you some of the details involved in the Father's Protective Presence and the means with which it will be manifested in the crisis hour for the children of God. It is well to trust in the general principle that, 'come what may, God will take care of me.' It is even more comforting to be apprised of His method and His Plan for doing so. Many have long walked by faith, believing but not seeing. This faith now finds its fruit within this body of practical revelation as it applies to the physical octave.

"In the darkest hour that can come for this planet, when its very existence would be destroyed were it not for the intervention of the Father's Hand, the millions who have dared to trust in Him when they had no other evidence other than their own faith, will be rewarded openly by being lifted into His Ark of Safety. As a hen gathereth her chicks under her wings, this ark provided will be the great armadas of floating cities that orbit the Earth on their MISSION OF MERCY!

"All of the units of heaven have laboured together on this great Plan, counciled together and served earnestly to bring to consummation the greatest rescue of souls of all time. The beloved sons and daughters of God *will* be hidden under our wings until the planet Earth is once more inhabitable. Then that which has been 'plucked up' shall be 'planted again,' and the Earth shall bring forth beautiful fruit in the Father's Name, within the cleansed and purified vibrations of a new heaven and a new Earth. Do not despair that others are not telling the story. The world has not been ready to hear. Many, at least, are close to the facts, though they know it not. But once again,

74

through this means, we who guard your world now tell unto man that which is before him. Let him choose wisely his response to the Plan.

"I am Kuthumi, World Teacher of this Solar System under the auspices of the Great Central Sun Government."

* * *

With these beautiful words to strengthen the "hope that is within us," we will be considering in this second part of our book, the planetary situation and the solution.

* * *

There is much concern throughout the Ashtar Command concerning the fear of mankind toward the peace-loving and goodwill ambassadors from outer space. Commander Ashtar speaks:

"I speak for the Most High Command of the Guardian Forces. Preparations are now underway for a great conclave of the Guardian Action. The masses must somehow be reached with an understanding of our true mission and the purpose of our presence in your skies. All fear must be removed from their hearts through teachings that will help them to understand that we surround your planet only in an attitude of love and helpfulness and a desire to serve mankind. Fear of us makes it impossible for the completion of our mission when the time is come.

"There are too many who fear us, too many who would withdraw and hold back should an invitation be given to come with us for rescue. We recognize the problem. We are dealing with it in every possible way through hundreds of precious willing souls Earth-based. We cannot be of help to those who fear us, who do not trust us, and who cannot accept us. The attitude of humanity must be changed for the great majority, before the hour of crisis. We cannot fulfill the Plan of the Hierarchy or assist mankind unless the world is enlightened to our

75

purpose and mission."

* * *

Beloved St. Germain has also contributed a message for sharing here:

"The massive buildup of negative effluvia surrounding the planet is being penetrated by our special cosmic rays to loosen and dissolve it. This will take considerable time, but the process is in action. These great rays have been sent forth from the Great Central Sun and will be in effect for the next three to five years. The solar system is now being slowly turned toward its new orbit and the Aquarian field of expression. When this is accomplished, the frequencies of Earth will be compatible with the rest of its system.

"We of the Solar Tribunal, who guard and watch over these events, have undertaken to release many from their heavy loads of remaining karma in order to assist them in turning towards the Light in these crucial times. The karmic patterns have been broken up for many through the decrees of the sons of Light, as well as the power of many avatars now in embodiment who do have that authority to remove or lessen the karma of a soul.

"In the future months for the world, we will begin to see a tremendous turning towards the Light and a marked increase of Light activities. These will be blessed and helped in a manner unprecedented. For all that is of the Light is now manifesting abundance of freedom and power, while simultaneously, those activities which are opposed to that Light are being drained of their energies and weakened in influence. Therefore, between the time that these specially trained envoys return to their places and that time when souls must be lifted, there will be a phenomenal growth in understanding and awareness all over the globe.

"This will be pressured into being partly by the ministry of these Earth-based Leaders, as it is combined with the incoming rays. The testimonies will be more acceptable than heretofore. Through the great rays the Spiritual Hierarchy will be active in the program. We all work in unison and with one mind and one goal for the uplifting of humanity. Both incarnate and discarnate Beings of Light will labor side by side in this great ingathering, while 'there is yet day' before 'the night cometh when none can work.'

"I leave my electronic presence with all who read these words, and my benediction rests upon them. I am St. Germain, of the Violet Ray."

* * *

For nearly two years, Guardian Action Publications has been distributing, with consistent success, a book compiled by Winfield Brownell, called *UFOs—KEYS TO EARTH'S DESTINY.* We have his permission and cooperation to reprint here a current message received by him from Monka, whose words we are always eager to hear:

"We have many many ships that are going through your atmosphere at all times; and now and then, here and there, we are helping more people to experience sightings of the ships, and some are being taken for trips. There is more of this type of activity, but it is just incidental. We are looking forward to the time when we can LAND in great numbers. We cannot land as long as too many Earth beings have *fear.* The condition of your feeling world is our test to tell whether or not we should bring in the ships in large numbers and land, before the serious cataclysmic activities or some other upset on Earth may come about.

"WE can test the feeling world of humankind, and judge exactly the level of its development. At the present time the percentage of your people who have more fear than WE would want to cause, is about six percent. Now the question is, how low must that percent register before we could take a chance on landing in large numbers? We feel that if it goes down below three percent, we can land in quite large numbers.

"We would experiment with it, if the number got down to that point. However, the percentage has not been lowering very much, so we hope there will be an improvement.

"There are more people in certain areas who would allow fear, and in this regard, your United States is a little bit lower than some of the other places because of experience and more publicity about UFOs, but you are still not down to three percent.

"We have been preventing your Earth from going into a flip on the axis, which would change the positions of your polar regions by displacing your equator. Such a displacement cataclysm would practically wipe out most of the life on Planet Earth; and if we needed to do this, *we would just withdraw the help which we have been giving, TO HOLD YOUR WORLD IN ORBIT.* Should it become necessary to withdraw our help, your planet would go into the flip on the axis, which in turn would soon end a war of any kind, and wash the whole Earth, and begin its purification.

"If that happened, it would only be a matter of minutes— an hour at the most—during which *we can pick up the persons to be saved.* There are almost 13,000,000 space ships close to your Earth now. Most are still in the liner dimension, so you do not see them. However, we can shift into another dimension which would be closer to your third dimension—close enough so we could pick up all of you beloved, precious ones in your physical bodies, and save those of you who would be proper to populate the Earth in the New Age, when you will have 'Heaven on Earth.'

"Work on your feeling world so that you are always at peace. Do not become disturbed. A disturbed climate would be dangerous if suddenly this activity of Earth's flip on the axis took place. Do not let anything IN to disturb you. If someone started an atomic war, or earthquakes, hurricanes or violence of that nature appeared, inner disturbance and fear would endanger you. Without fear, you are protected by the Light which you have drawn about you, and the greater Light which you continue to draw.

"Sad to relate, as the energies are stepped up and frequencies increased, the evil forces are more active. They are in their last throes, as it were, and some of them are getting desperate. They feel that they may not be able to accomplish their mission in controlling others to promote undesirable deeds. Their desperation has caused them to step up evil happenings, and the evil is receiving more publicity."

* * *

Monka's closing paragraph brings to mind further words in the message from Andromeda Rex through messenger Lucy Colson:

"Those of you who are Light Commanders must be brought further into our radiation and thoughts. Now is the time in which we call you to attend to your duties for which you were posted into an early lifetime. Arise, O Eagles, arise and fly that Michael and His Hosts may join you in flushing from the Earth all vestiges of evil and negativity. The planet Earth must return to its rightful place in the Cosmos."

* * *

A prominent leader of the Intergalactic Fleet, Commander Alphon, speaking through messenger Lyara, of Golden Rays Center in Phoenix, reveals:

"Each soul has already been locked into the coordinates for their unique timing and circumstances. Rest assured that planetary evacuation is quite familiar to us, and each detail has been fully accounted for. Those involved are being prepared at conscious and unconscious levels. The existing energies of the core of this planet will be gradually releasing in vast magnitude, eventually rendering its surface temporarily unusable. It is not only the physical changes, but resulting boomerangs, that will affect the quality and survival of life here. It is still scheduled that an estimated ten percent are scheduled for departure. The remainder will not have a long opportunity to support life at this dimension. The severity will assist souls' release from the third dimension quite rapidly.

"Each of you who are scheduled to relocate will be assisted rapidly to do so. Each will be in his/her proper location soon. Assemble supplies for self-sufficiency dependent on your unique directions. Gather water purifiers, food, bedding, and other essentials. Earth must karmically fulfill certain destinies and plans. Recognize that just as your destiny is to serve in these final days, others are on different courses of destiny. Be true to the Godself within. Love, Alphon, of the Intergalactic Fleet."

Another release From Alphon through Lyara continues, "Evacuation plans have already been initiated through natural planetary disasters and disappearances, and will become increasingly evident. Many pickup points coordinated by each sector will make a gradual and peaceful, planned departure of Earth's citizens in addition to those taken through disappearance and natural disaster events.

"There are many reasons for this acceleration. First is the inaccuracy of the present day calendar system, which is off by thirteen years. Then, there has been planetary vibrational acceleration caused by several Factors, including atomic research testing. The third and the final reason that both the surface and middle earth must be evacuated, is the planetary lineup, followed quickly by the bypass a larger planet.

"Approximately ten percent of the planetary population is to be taken aboard for eventual return to the planet after 5 to 7 years. Some will remain aboard ships. The boarding pass for all will be 'love in the aura,' for without that, one cannot withstand the higher vibrational frequencies which will be necessary.

"Items of spiritual value and advanced technology which have been guarded by the brotherhoods, will be withdrawn and replaced when the planet is repopulated."

* * *

In early August my own Commander spokesman brought in to me, a Great Commander who comes from a very high-ranking station in the Ashtar Command, a great Leader honored by all. He truly exemplifies the spirit of Love. He is the Record Keeper for the Galaxy and the records are kept on the planet bearing his name. It was my great privilege to welcome HATONN to contribute to this book:

"Fellow citizens of planet Earth, I bring you my thoughts on the plight of your planet. We look down upon it and see within its inner being the record of all of its turmoils throughout all of its history. We see the struggles of the Light to shine forth and the hindering influences of the dark ones. We observe and we wait, knowing that ultimately the Earth will be as a great shining star, the most beautiful in all the heavens. Why would you seek to destroy it, O man? Cannot your differences be reconciled in a peaceful way?

"We of the outer worlds have found a way to do this, and have learned that Love is the only way toward peace and enjoyment of our brothers. There were times eons ago when some of our worlds had not yet found this solution. In their torment and thrust for power over others, they did also seek the great weapons of destruction and did cause much havoc within many constellations. Their greed and lust for power and control of other worlds only led to the destruction of themselves. There is an eternal monument to them seen as the stardust fragments across the heavens. Out of these problems, we of the Galactic Federation of Planets formed the Galactic Pact, which forbids warfare against another, and the warlike ones who would not yield were removed from our midst.

"Now your world has projected itself into this chaotic time of unrest and threat due to the calculations of a few in your midst who will not yield to the peaceful way or the attitude of peace and love on Earth. This is regrettable, for your entire solar system is destined to orbit its way into a higher fre-

81

quency manifestation. This will lift your entire world into vibrations so elevated that only the peaceful man may survive in them. Therefore, it is ordained that before this orbit into the Golden Age is fulfilled, the Earth will be prepared for its advancement by many changes. War will be removed, outlawed, from your planet, and all of the impurities of your way of life will be filtered away by the changing scene due to begin. There will be much turmoil in your midst and much sorrow for those who have sought to instigate bloodshed upon Terra.

"We, therefore, have been authorized by the Spiritual Hierarchy, to intervene in the affairs of Earth in the event of attempted nuclear holocaust. This will not be permitted by the higher intelligences who watch over your affairs. Intervention will come to you in the form of cataclysms of great magnitude. We plead with mankind, yet this day, to lay aside your arms and dismantle your stockpiles of death, and come to the peace tables to settle your differences. Come in the desire to find another way. Know there is a better way and labor together until you find it. Lean not upon your military powers, but rather, look to the Most High for your directions. Even in this book, designed to warn you of the coming Evacuation and what to expect concerning it, I nevertheless plead with humanity, and I say this can yet be avoided if man will change and turn his eyes toward God. The Love of God within all men must be allowed to express itself and space must be made in your thinking for its outworking in your international affairs.

"Nevertheless, having stated thus, I do now give my attention to the peacemakers among you. Your efforts are carefully recorded and every effort of love to extend love amongst your Fellows shall not be forgotten, but your reward shall come to you. Further, you will *not be expected to be a participant* in the destructions you have labored so faithfully TO AVERT. You will be removed from the chaos and be sheltered in our ships that will come to escort you to safety. I have many times visualized this great event in my mind, marvelling at the efficiency of the Plan and the expertise of those who will bring it to completion.

"Many of you who read these words will be assisting us from the ground level in this great undertaking. As above, so below. The teamwork of cooperative effort will prepare souls in advance and acclimate them when the zero hour has come. The primary purpose for sending forth this document by the Ashtar Command is to prepare the minds of those enlightened souls now present upon the planet with at least a veiled description of what to expect at these crucial events, and thus, lessen the presence of fear.

"Therefore, I sum up for your consideration some basic statements to hold in your mental storehouse against that hour:

1. Each of your names is written down on the records held in our great computers. Your sectors are carefully assigned to certain fleets and Commanders who oversee the needs of your sector. *WE KOW YOU ARE THERE AND EXACTLY WHERE YOU ARE.*

2. Each one of you will without fail receive definite instructions at crisis moment so that you will know where to be at a given time. No one will be missed or overlooked, and your participation is sure.

3. Units of families, separated in the great exodus, will be brought together again on our ships as soon as events make this possible. Do not harbor fear of any kind, but think only in an attitude of thankfulness to Our Father.

4. There will be some you know and whom you love who will be remaining behind for reasons built into their own being. You must release them into the hands of the Father, who will receive their spiritual being into His House where there are many mansions. They will be escorted to a place their inner thoughts and life patterns have created for them, to begin again their upward spiral. You must accept that their personal choices have created their personal destiny.

5. There will be a natural missing of accustomed environment, but a brief time with us will bring a forgetfulness, as you settle into the new routines and surrounding atmosphere. Our ships are beautiful places to be, and the atmosphere within them is joy and love and concern for one another. There will be those of your own, already trained to assist you in your adjustment to your new environment. We will have trained these beforehand for the work they are to do.

6. You will recognize and know these leaders as special representatives of our mission, even before the crisis has come. Follow them and heed their instructions, that all may go smoothly for you at the time of great confusion.

"I am Hatonn, and I shall personally greet all of you when you are lifted into our midst to remain with us for a little while. When your planet has been healed, you will be returned to it and all of your needs for reconstruction will be given. Higher Intelligences shall walk with you to assist you in a speedy reclaiming of the Earth in Universal Love. I am grateful for your consideration of my words."

(Dear Hatonn, how grateful we all are for your helpful guidance.)

* * *

We are living in a time when we must develop and become efficient in the operation of our own personal guidance system. No longer should we run to this one and that one and another for confirmation and details or answers to our questions. Some will take a book and go to a half dozen other souls to find out if that messenger is valid. Who is to say that the other is more valid in his guidance system than that one who seeks him? Look to the God within and learn to function independently as an outpost of the Divine. In all of the confusion of compilation from stacks of messages, we have misplaced the name of the speaker of the following paragraph, but we are indebted to

Lyara for the message:

"You will board our ships as your frequency permits. Your children and ours will play together and learn from each other within the Cosmic Family. Refinement will be essential, for within rapid changes each soul will have to be tuned to the cosmic station we are operating on to know where to be and what to be doing each moment. There will *not be time to consult with another for guidance;* you must be working at a feeling, hearing, or seeing level with the within—preferably all three."

In a joint statement to Lyara from Hilarion, St. Germain and Cetti, this message comes:

"Mass preparations of evacuation of this planet are being made by the fleets. Not only are preparations at a maximum speed being made for proper evacuation, but also for *withdrawal from all command stations within the planet!* It is a momentous task preparing on all levels for the needs of the citizens of Earth and also, the acceptance and preparations with the citizens through the inner universe. *Each of you reading this,* at conscious or unconscious levels, are supporting these activities and etherically rapidly creating more structures, pictures, activities, plans for successful transition. In addition, you are sitting in on meetings and classes to prepare yourselves vibrationally and spiritually for the days to come. Stay tuned to the inner. Remain calm and centered. Not only will activities be done from the 'right' vibration, but you will conserve your energy for increased productivity.

"Each minute, hour, and day it will become apparent to you what your proper activities are to be. *There are no accidents or coincidences. There is only right action!* In the immediate future acceleration will be phenomenal, so keep all commitments on as short a range as possible. Commit to transitional activities, but do not make specific dates for events too far ahead.

"The Earth will rumble, and the fires will pour forth.

85

Those who stand upon the rock of Truth will be secure. Trust that within the Love of God all things are provided for."

A vast portion of the Intergalactic League of Special Volunteers are with us in the status of a "walk-in" soul who has come to occupy the physical form of another who no longer desires to retain its form on this physical plane. A very lucid passage discussing this phenomenon was received by a dear friend and beautiful channel, Bettina Kramer. Her source is a feminine entity from the seventh plane who is one of Bettina's regular Higher Teachers. Bettina retold the message to me, and I am passing along the information in my own words.

It seems that these entities who enter our dimension as walk-ins are highly trained for their mission. They have completed in-depth training and all have a tremendous Love for all of humanity. They must, of course, make up certain things in their own past karma, and the entire experience is not an easy one for them. When they accept a physical vehicle they must adjust and fit themselves into that new form, however uncomfortable it may be for them. Often, many uncomfortable feelings accompany this process. Further, they are also responsible to work out the works that the departing person leaves undone. These preliminary or accompanying responsibilities are additional to the special work the walk-in has come to accomplish.

Each one is fully versed in the work that one has come to do. They are largely more enlightened than the Earth-born volunteers, because they can see both the past and the future— backwards and forwards. However, some do not awaken immediately. For example, they may continue for a time in a dazed state, and proceed slowly to a full awareness. But in time, they all are endowed with the ability of contacting the higher planes of tremendous knowledge and wisdom. If a certain walk-in is a little delayed in awakening to the mission undertaken, another walk-in is directed to him. Only a soul with the walk-in status is capable of discerning another of like status.

Many will claim to be a walk-in through ego, confusion, or misinformation, but if one truly is a walk-in, he does not discuss it or refer to it at any time. They simply do not discuss it. As the Teacher explained, "It isn't the time, and when it is the time, they will be too busy to talk about it."

The person who voluntarily desires to vacate the body, through weariness of life, loss of the will to live, or whatever cause, is permitted to depart from the physical vehicle and release it to the walk-in soul. However, that departing person thoroughly understands that at some point in the future it must make up every bit of its karma that has been left unbalanced at departure. The same problems must be faced upon returning. Nothing has been escaped, only postponed, but the soul has at least been generous enough to surrender the form to another who will carry through Earth responsibilities. Many, at the moment of surrender, become frightened and require special assistance.

Walk-ins are always very beautiful people, highly advanced in spiritual abilities. They may have their human faults as do all, and may have inherited flaws, but because of their tremendous willingness to be present on the planet, they are magnetic souls.

The persons that depart the vehicle have no debt against them for having done this, beyond the existing personal debt to their own soul. They are aware they will have to repeat the round again.

The entering walk-in experiences normal physical death in the manner of any earthling. Of course, he will be a candidate for the physical changeover to a Light body as well as any earthling, but in normal times the walk-in ends his time here in the same manner as others. They cannot "come and go" as it were, but are anchored within their chosen physical form as any other incarnate. They have accepted the mission with that understanding. All serve toward the uplifting of humanity and the increase of Light upon the planet.

* * *

Truly, the "Mission of Mercy" to our little globe is beyond the scope of human understanding.

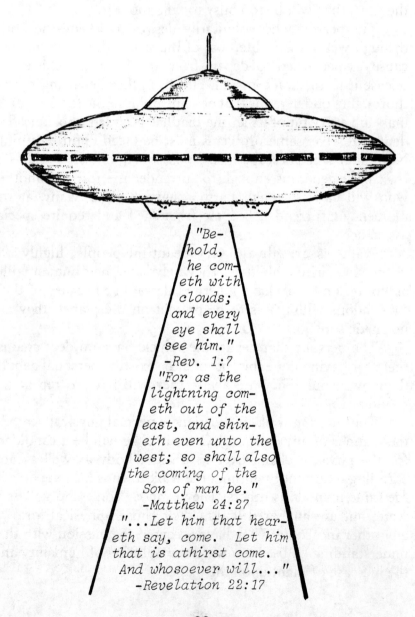

"Be-
hold,
he com-
eth with
clouds;
and every
eye shall
see him."
-Rev. 1:7
"For as the
lightning com-
eth out of the
east, and shin-
eth even unto the
west; so shall also
the coming of the
Son of man be."
-Matthew 24:27
"...Let him that hear-
eth say, come. Let him
that is athirst come.
And whosoever will..."
-Revelation 22:17

The Gathering Storm

Probably one of the most important releases this year from the Guardians of our planet, relative to nuclear warfare, came in a joint statement by Joshua, of the Spiritual Hierarchy, and Andromeda Rex, high in the echelons of Universal Statesmanship and the Space Alliance. The statement deals with "The Effect of Nuclear Attack upon the Soul," through the spiritual messengership of Lucy Colson:

"It is very disruptive to the soul's growth to encounter the full nuclear radiation resulting from global conflict. One tends to believe that the four lower bodies are separated by time and space. This is not true. What happens to the physical body during a nuclear attack affects the non-physical bodies as well.

"The soul can most definitely be affected; and any nuclear attack is an attack upon the soul of others—military targets notwithstanding. The nuclear effect affects the auric envelope around a person, and according to how close the person is to the blast area, it can either maim the envelope permanently or destroy it completely. Normally those whose energy fields are thusly affected die in a very short period—not so much from the radiation, which is, of course, poisonous to the human organism, but because the Light or Life of the person is destroyed. It is this Light—the Very Light of Very Life—which is a person's connection, or Life-Line between dimensions. This Light—or energy—travels along the Golden Cord.

"What is the Golden Cord? In the interior of the Silver Cord is a Golden Cord filled with a golden vital energy, vital to

89

the person because it is this Light energy descending through the cord which keeps the person alive. Once the physical is destroyed, the problem has only begun. The Spirit is released through the Silver Cord, but in nuclear death, not in the normal way as when the cord is snapped and withdrawn from the person.

"Life is energy, regardless of what dimension the person is in. Energy can become distorted as various factors play upon it. It is this distortion, brought about by the nuclear blast and subsequent radiation, which concerns us now. The distortion causes the soul to suffer inordinately. There is a warping of the life energy at several planes of consciousness which must be dealt with. It takes a great deal of care and patience to realign a soul once it has been subjected to this ordeal. While most of our methods are not understandable to the Earth plane at this time, you might say that we have to polarize the energy fields of the soul before it can go on to its rightful domain.

"We have had to deal with this several times upon your planet. Unfortunately, these destructive rays are not unique to your planet and the effects have been felt elsewhere in the solar system at various times. However, once a ban was proclaimed, all other planetary systems abided by the conditions set forth in the agreement, realizing the terrible damage that is done to the soul. Your planet is now the only one not in accordance with the Galactic agreement on the use of so-called nuclear energies. We fear for your peoples. As we have mentioned, we cannot interfere UNLESS there is TOTAL nuclear destruction indicated—and then we interfere because the soul's purpose warrants interruption of the life form on the planet. We cannot interfere for anything less than a soul-threatening event, unless specifically advised to do so by your own Planetary Hierarchy."

* * *

The following bold statement was made by Space Master Monka in his message through Winfield Brownell:

"WE HAVE PROMISED THAT WE WILL NOT ALLOW AN ATOM BOMB WAR TO GAIN ANY MOMENTUM SUFFICIENT TO CAUSE SEVERE RADIOACTIVITY ON YOUR PLANET. You have enough already, from the bombs dropped experimentally and otherwise, which is sad to relate. This is the great crime against humanity! All atomic activity should cease upon the Earth. THERE IS NO SAFE WAY of taking care of the waste material from the nuclear plants which are creating so much of it, using plutonium and other radioactive substances. Expansion of these nuclear plants is in error, and very undesirable. Also, THERE IS NO SAFE WAY IN WHICH RADIOACTIVE MATERIALS CAN BE USED. If you carried on with an all-out atom bomb war to the detriment of other planets, we can prevent the war from continuing. Under certain circumstances we could even *prevent an individual from ever pushing the button* to start an atomic war!"

* * *

That was a striking statement to me, for I now dare to share with you information which is evidential of this type of intervention. This account was allegedly obtained by an unnamed aerospace engineer from a participant in the events related. For very obvious reasons, the engineer must remain anonymous. The account is repeated verbatim.

"The incident took place a few years ago at a tactical atomic missile battery in Europe near the Eastern border. An unidentified target appeared at extreme range on the radar sonar net: initially exhibiting the electronic characteristics of a ferret, a spy mission to seek out and study enemy radar, radio, and other electromagnetic emissions. As if realizing that it had been detected, the unknown blip quickly began to respond in imitation of friendly aircraft. After routine correlation of data, the evaluation center serving the missile battery initiated a red alert. Missile #1 was raised from its stowed position and readied for launch. Missile #2 was alerted to back up status. Missile

91

#3 was alerted to standby status. At the point in missile #1's countdown, where the system dictated a built-in hold to prevent unauthorized launch, the system failed.

"It was a human failure. The firing officer on missile #1 was known among his fellow soldiers as a hot-headed right winger whose personal formula for world peace was complete destruction of all communists, the sooner the better. Evidently feeling that he would never be confronted with a better excuse, he pushed the firing button that would start World War III. However, instead of a missile lift-off, he got a red malfunction on his display console, followed immediately by a bullet through his brain, fired by a security officer posted behind him to prevent such things.

"The missile automatically lowered to its stowed position in its launcher, missile #2 was alerted from back-up status to launch-ready status, missile #3 was alerted to backup status from standby. Before missile #2 had proceeded half way from its alert towards its built-in hold in the countdown, it, too, displayed a red malfunction light and lowered to its stowed position. Missile #3 had barely started its countdown when the red light appeared on the display panel. The *UNIDENTIFIED* cause of it all reversed its course and departed out of range.

"All three missiles, their launchers, and associated equipment, controls and displays, were completely dismantled and inspected, to find the three separate malfunctions that had been indicated. There were none! The equipment was new and in perfect condition. Army Intelligence was called in and interviewed all personnel thoroughly. It was noticed that the investigators did not seem to think that the incident *was at all unusual* or warranted any skepticism. It was as if *it had all happened many times before!* It might be expected that in an event with such profound implications concerning the history of the human race, the prospects for peace, and the degree to which the human race controls its destiny, would have its effects on the outlook of the participants, even if they were not allowed to divulge the facts.

"Indeed, the effects on the second firing officer seemed most beneficial. His intelligence seemed to increase markedly. He became outgoing, cheerful, and much happier than before. When promised anonymity, he divulged the reason behind his transformation. The unknown target was a UFO, so-called. On board the alien craft was a sophisticated energy and data-storing system, far beyond any computer Earth has yet envisioned. Its function is to store the extremely complex intelligent energy entity people incompletely refer to by such terms as 'consciousness,' 'ego,' or 'soul.' This is done when the entity's physical body dies. During the encounter between the missile battery and the UFO, contact was established between the entity in the UFO and the second missile firing officer. Permission to take over control and occupancy of the officer's body was negotiated, requested and granted. The alien entity was then transmitted into the officer by a directed energy beam. In this case of visitation, the alien left virtually all of his memories behind, which are functioning with the officer's memories, and at a tremendously high level of awareness, capability and intelligence. The officer has since left the military, but is employed by one of the nation's largest aerospace contractors."

I have since destroyed the tape received from which this transcript was prepared, so that I would no longer have any evidential trace to my informant in my possession. I chose to share it with you because the incident clearly reveals to us one manner of outside intervention when the threat of nuclear holocaust is present.

* * *

My mail is constantly filled with interesting things from concerned world citizens alerted in their desire to assist the Ashtar Command in its overtures for planetary peace. My informant in the following letter lives on the coastal region of southern California. He writes:

"Between 12:00 noon and 1:00 p.m. Saturday, July 24, 1982, I received a radio message which I believe was transmitted by the Ashtar Communications Command. It came through on the AM frequency of 10,000 kHz so strong that it blanked out the regular programming which transmits at a power of 10,000 watts of output. I do not know whether it was a broad band or a fixed beam.

"I am aware that Ashtar messages can be transmitted on many different frequencies for as long as twenty-four to seventy-two hours at a time, and many times these messages can be received over a television set, an electronic oven, and over the telephone. Because of this, it is my opinion that the Ashtar Transmitter is operating at around one million watts on carrier wave, which is not legal in America, for the most power our stations are allowed to use is 50,000 watts. Logically, to me, the only other place this extremely powerful signal could come from was the Ashtar Command vehicle.

"Unfortunately, I did not hear the signing of the message as the vehicle moved outside my receiver range at 1:00 p.m., at which time the regular program returned. That portion of the message I did clearly receive was of the Very High Authority and did concern actions of today around the world in general, and in the Middle East in particular, more of an informing nature rather than a warning. It is my understanding that there have been three warning messages received in this manner to date, and I understand there will be no more of these to come. Six messages such as I received that day have been received from these Higher Authorities but none of them have been acknowledged by today's world governments. Part of these warning messages stressed the need for both Russia and America to stay clear of Israel's contest for survival, or risk intervention by extraterrestrial forces."

* * *

The following discourse was one of those received for the

book while still in Utah this summer. Contact was established with a greatly beloved Commander, named Korton, of the Communications Network of this Solar System.

"We of the communications system headquarters located on Mars, constantly monitor all communications that are transmitted throughout the Ashtar Command as well as all communications received or sent forth to or from our representatives, channels and messengers present on Earth. It gives me great pleasure once again to administer to you a few thoughts which may be a somewhat worthy contribution to this coming effort.

"In the beginning of this decade, as the Great Council convened to discuss planetary affairs, much heaviness filled our hearts.

"The situation existing in and around and upon the planet was crucial, because of the evil ministrations and the dark intentions of certain ones embodied in your midst. These dark ones desire to instigate world situations which would produce chaos and disorder within the Earth family and result in tremendous unnecessary loss of life from this platform of evolution. Growth and evolvement would be disrupted for many souls, as well as ultimately defeating the Glory of God intended to fill Earth with Love and Grace.

We have known the utmost effort to this end would be extended by this group of whom I speak. The ultimate goal is nuclear war and destruction of the present prevailing economic system. The final idea of enslavery of mankind and total subjection of humanity to the ruling few would result in total extinction of freedom of will and man's right of choice to determine his pathway. As embodied sparks of the divine, this choice is their inherent right, ordained at creation. The tenets of Universal Law prevail in all of the solar system and galaxies of this universe. We have therefore been given the authority to intervene and to interrupt, disrupt and destroy these plans to enslave souls. The Spiritual Hierarchy has ordained total freedom to us in these matters. We have considered the hostilities internationally, the threats of escalation that appear almost constantly and the issues as we see them. It is evident that a master diabolical hand prepares these ever-recurring incidents, skirmishes of lesser scale, military hostile actions and the repeated disturbances in one small nation after another.

"We are alert to the 'beast' and the plan and the purpose of the plan. We are united in our love for your world, with freedom to choose your own pathway within your own guidance system. Presently, many karmic debts remain upon nations which must be reconciled. However, we continue aloof to those situations where karmic debt is a factor, until that point in circumstances when the Great Law is fulfilled. Beyond that point, intervention by the Intergalactic Confederation forces will be forthcoming, and men shall be told their acts aggression shall proceed this far and no farther. The destiny of this planet may not be destroyed.

"Military offenses of whatever nature are monitored by our Commands, and close discernment of karmic patterns is faithfully examined. When national situations reach a boiling point, some nuclear activity can be expected within the karmic concept, but wanton uncontrolled destruction will precipitate our intervention under Universal Law. At the point of national and personal accountability, all nuclear action will cease, by use of our technology.

"The capability of mankind to make right choices is in a continual changing pattern, and in many areas greatly changing for the better. Consequently, we cannot offer dates and times and specifics involved. The element of constant change affects prophecy of the past, from or through any source, including your scriptures. These which deal with international affairs are subject to the will of man and his desire to find solutions in love.

"In our assessment of affairs, it seems unlikely that world evacuation would be precipitated by warfare. World evacuation has primarily been planned because of threats from other sources. I refer to the spiritual evolvement of humanity or the lack of it, and the influence it brings to bear upon the Life Force of the entity Earth. The aspirations of its inhabitants determine its destiny, as well as their own. Disharmony brings destruction. Displacement of spiritual values effects displacement of matter within and upon the globe of Terra. Earth changes will be the primary factor in mass evacuation of this planet. We will be standing by while the entity Earth's efforts to protect itself, shakes off its irritants and destructive elements.

"There is no place for fear of any kind relating to these matters. Everyone whose understanding has this awareness of our constant vigil on your behalf, who understands that the Heavenly Father knoweth the whereabouts of each of His Own and that the very hairs of your heads are numbered, should feel secure. We speak of the children of Light. The planet entity will enter a period of cleansing to prepare itself for its Golden Age. You are a part of that heritage and you shall inherit the Earth and its glory. This is Korton, of Mars, speaking for the Ashtar Command."

* * *

"Masters who can read the Akashic Records have stated that China will soon have enough atomic and hydrogen bombs to start a war for the subjugation, under them, of everyone else on Earth. Perhaps so, but the insight that has made its way throughout New Age circles has it that the cause for the comparatively recent unprecedented earthquake in China was the massive secret underground military installation there, covertly concealing the housing of untold thousands of troops geared for offensive action.

"They boast of tomorrow" like that one who proposed to "build many new barns," totally unaware of the true state of things as they are and as they will be! The brotherhood of man

97

is a reality, for Our Father has "made of one blood all nations …on Earth…and determined the times before appointed, and the bounds of their habitation." (Acts 17:26) No other commandment has been given that is greater than the admonition to love our neighbors as we love ourselves! Love is the circumspection and the completion of all Universal Law. For "being rooted and grounded in love," we can comprehend the "breadth, length, and depth and height" of the inner divinity, or splendor, within every man!

* * *

Into the heaviness of thought at this point in the book, beloved J.W., of Jupiter, came bounding in like the clean gust of a fresh wind:

"Many years ago according to your Earth's time, it was my privilege to give to the world a small volume entirely dictated by me, through a channel called Gloria Lee. Essentially my message then contained descriptions and details dealing with the identical subject of this book. The former book was withdrawn out of print with the translation of my channel, and I have not attempted another like discourse since that time. However, the book remained to fulfill its ministry in triggering the awakening of many of the Special Volunteers upon the Earth. So it did serve its purpose to the few to whom it was sent.

"Now it is a great joy to me to learn of this project of the Ashtar Command in producing this volume so necessary in this day. Again I realize, it is sent to the few, just as mine was in its day. Nevertheless, this outreach is of great importance to the Commands. The fleets of Jupiter and many others are occupied in their assignment on the other side of your world, but we desire to bring you this word to assure you that we shall assist in distribution of these words throughout Europe, the Orient and all points surrounding them. This will be our contributing effort and every fleet in my charge hails this mission of beloved

Kuthumi and Commander Ashtar.

"I desire to leave a brief message to those souls into whose hands this volume will be placed. Now is the hour! Now is the time! Look not for another decade or even the completion of this one. We have in our responsibility the presence of many nations who are not content to live in peace, but whose appetites for world power would destroy all that lies in their pathway if that were possible. Our constant vigilance above them has been a saving grace in many threatening situations over here, but that does not insure that at any given moment a wrong button will not be pushed, or despair of solution instigate the first strike. There are those with diabolical plots to make it so. These we must watch with great concern. For it is not the people of these nations who act in this way, but the small cluster of certain ones in whose hands control is placed, who have the authority and the power to manipulate their circumstances which would lead to greater conflict.

"We are the silent watchers and we are the Guards! But it is like unto the lid of the pressure cooker which is about to burst forth its steam. Be not unbelieving of these pages, but know they are the truth; these are urgent things the enlightened ones must know and be prepared for. You can expect that within five years' time, this entire book will probably be fulfilled. Although I have been cautioned by those who oversee these messages, not to set dates or speak of time, yet I do dare to make this general conjecture, based on our reconnaissance here.

"Mankind cannot count upon time. We join with all of the Ashtar Command in admonishing those who have started upon the pathway of illumination to grasp the garment of truth and adorn thy being. Be love! Be light! Be in tune with the universe and its thrust for Light upon the planet Earth. All else is the way of the fool.

"Again I thank you for this opportunity to speak, and all of our help will be forthcoming to spread these messages. I am ever at your service, J.W. of Jupiter."

* * *

A paragraph from beloved Joshua, through messenger Lucy Colson, seems a fitting summary with which to close this section:

"While plans are going ahead for planetary evacuation, they are going ahead on a 'crisis basis' only. Man, with his Free Will, has the option to stay the Hand of the Lord. While the hour is extremely late, we have not given up hope that man will yet realize the immediacy of his peril, both to himself and his planet, and come into alignment with his Christ Being. However, should there be planetary warfare, then the Hand of God will be stayed no more, and we will have to rescue our Light Servers, for theirs is not the destiny to witness the full cleansing."

The Cleansing Action

Earth's axis is influenced by the weight of the karma of humanity. Man's inhumanity to man and voluminous thought forms and feelings of negative emotions have tipped the axis of the planet. Electrons have weight—though very slight, singly, of tremendous heaviness in the aggregate. It has been pointed out that this has been concentrated mostly in the northern hemisphere and has bent the axis. This bend of the axis causes instability in earth's revolving action.

Churchwood's books on "Mu" graphically describe this tipping, producing colossal tidal waves of water, gravel, and ice, destroying all life in its pathway. Earth's proper climates can only be restored to normal in the arighting of the axis. In the halls of heaven we are told there are blueprints for planet Earth which present the original designed continental distribution of the earth. Originally the seven continents encircled the globe at its greatest diameter, while water occupied the other two regions. To restore the original continental distribution will require tremendous cataclysmic activity, sinking certain continents beneath the seas and raising others.

Following this, the barren earth would need proper climate restoration and a new covering of foliage and vegetation.

Spiritual Light Being Lytton mentions this (through Lyara):

"The physical earth is a living organism/ consciousness, and is continuously being created by group consciousness. Solidified thought forms have densified into rocks, earth, insti-

101

tutions, and constructions, etc., which must be broken up to yield to new vibrations and new creations. From the higher vibration will emerge the new heaven and the new earth. The entire surface of the planet will be reconstructed."

Lytton has important things to say concerning acceleration also:

"The significant activity in the 1970's that had such an *impact* upon time was the *ATOMIC UNDERGROUND BLASTS!* Each human life form is composed of millions of atoms. It is the lowest visible, divisible structure to our physical world. Within the atom exists the exact counterpart of the outer universe—the inner universe. It is not visible by human senses or instruments, for like its constituents, it can only be perceived by spiritual vision or, in some cases, by properties. The science of etherons is one application of the principles of the 'stuff' composing the atom.

"The rate the atom vibrates in matter constitutes the uniqueness of the creation the thought form supports. For example, a rock vibrates quite slowly, whereas man, depending upon his spiritual/soul development, can vibrate quite rapidly.

"All on this planet share a common substance of space which surrounds the atoms. Through this space flows the life force which connects *all creations* on or within this planet. Now what do you imagine happens when *man splits the atomic structure violently in one part of the surface of the planet, or within?* The Life Force which flows through the ether (as rapidly as your thoughts are sent into the universe—instantly) and *all atomic structures begin to accelerate in their vibration, causing TIME, as vibration, to accelerate, PUTTING US MANY YEARS INTO THE FUTURE!* No more atomic blasting is allowed! You, as citizens of the earth, have already spiraled this planet into the last year! As the earth begins to yield to this pressure within and without, and the stars within the heavens exert *their* influences, rapid, imminent changes must occur. We, in the fleet, could not prevent you

102

from your destiny of bringing the planet into its final work, *but* we have *now* been allowed to oversee how you handle this. It is *not* allowed for you to blow up this planet, as Maldek and other planets have done when they developed nuclearly. We have given repeated warnings to your leaders. They have been ignored.

"Now we can only carefully monitor assisting with as many awakening projects as you have given yourselves time for, and safely evacuate those who are ready to go home with us. Obviously the current vibrational frequency acceleration has a profound effect upon life on the planet. People intuitively feel changes. Many are opening to new dimensions, but they do not understand what is going on. These anxiety/fearful thought forms will accelerate air and ether pollution to the sensitive, causing them to leave the cities or live together for personal evolution and work.

"It is the discordant conditions between these higher energies now hitting the planets and the fears and subsequent thought forms which people have created which are the true battle between light and dark forces, or the lower and higher which people have created. The *real war is within the souls* and hearts of every man on the planet."

* * *

Scientists have spoken of two enormous sunspots on the surface of the sun—presently dormant—that are the largest ever seen. But if they should flare, they would cause a magnitude of earth disturbances and earthquakes the like of which has never been known within a recorded time. There has also been much talk concerning a possible collision with Earth from another heavenly body. I asked my teacher, Kuthumi, concerning this, and he replied:

"This is a time-controlled event. The negative quality of Earth could magnetize it toward its location, but if the cleansing has already occurred for this planet, the other heavenly

103

body would be diverted from its course. If it comes coinciden-
tal with nuclear action, it would be permitted as another form
of cleansing."

* * *

This summer I was greatly moved by an account of the
stabilizing action of our beloved Brothers from Space, which
appeared in the *New Atlantean Journal,* and I am sharing it
here:

"An acquaintance of Hermann Ilg (contactee) who is
employed with a geological institute where also seismologic
surveying takes place, informed him that during the months of
January and February, 1982, an incredible observation has
been made: *There was not the slightest geological movement!*
The apparatuses did not show anything for weeks! This has
not been the case as long as the apparatuses are in action,
because the earth crust is in slight movement day after day. She
asked for an explanation from the Spheres of Light, and this
was the answer:

"The extraterrestrials detected at the end of 1981, an increasing, highly dangerous axial declination impending to
evoke a hyperchaotic condition. This is because of the rolling
motion. As an immediate counteraction, it was decided to
place all available mother ships around the whole planet in
such a way that this was approximately in keeping with the
meridians. Through the emission of their powerful radiant
energy, the earth was taken as into a vise. Thereby, the abnor-
mal rolling motion could be highly reduced, although not completely. Had this not been done, there would not be a pole
jump during the coming entry of the earth into the Monastic
vibration, as expected, but there would have been that pole
changing which would have led to a total devastation of our
planet in 1982. So you see that in late 1981 there was a highly
dangerous situation. But despite this stabilizing action, the
huge natural catastrophies will occur in late 1982, because the

lining up of the planets will then be terminated and will be more effective."'

"In the same issue of the *New Atlantean Journal,* Allan J. Grise mentioned that "scientists have announced the existence of the Great American Fault Line, a vast mega-crack in the earth's surface, that runs from Seattle all the way to the lower reaches of the Appalachians, some 1700 miles long and 90 miles wide at places, indicating that most of us now live near a major fault line."

* * *

More interesting and vital update concerning earth events comes to us in a joint statement from Lytton, St. Germain, and Cassion, through Lyara:

"Heavy releases of the plates of Mother Earth, movement and motions which previously would take many years to accomplish, will begin in vast motion. The triggers beneath the plates in Africa, Southern Europe, Mideast, Australia and the West Coast have been accomplished. Great patterns and flow of energies are occurring now at the subsurface levels the planet, propelling triggering actions and reactions to each event now, thousands of miles from the source. We can no longer stabilize fault lines, and indeed, it is no longer our position to do so.

"In your 'sleep' states many of you can recall working with earthquakes, volcanoes, energy lines, grid patterns and travel to various spots around the world. You are each a part of working groups differentiated by etheric colors (there's that color coordination again!) and are called to come together for service every night now. You are being provided an understanding at the soul level of changes which are occurring. Those on the birth path of Love balance dense emotional energies on the planet by the neutralizer of Love. Just as blocks of emotions prevent the proper flow of life force through the human body, so do collected thought forms block the flow of the conduit channels of energy flowing through continents and energy lines. Keep the energy in your abodes and activities high and stay tuned, unemotionally, to the channel of Divine Love, and you will always be guided in your activities and your decisions.

The release of energy from nuclear power plants will be one of our biggest concerns. Nuclear energy was definitely an example of giving toys to children. It has only sped up the transition for all the population. What was planned to be more gradual has now become accelerated because of the energies released and imbalances facilitated in both the etheric and physical life forces. We will not allow the entire planet to be destroyed. If atomic warfare does become activated, that will be the point of immediate mass evacuation by us of the prepared citizens of planet Earth.

"Earth changes this year will have far-reaching effects upon the nuclear power plants around the world. NONE are safe from potential leaks if given lethal impacts.

"Some unfortunately will not be closed in sufficient time to prevent damage to communities. Major earthquakes will cause fissures, with immediate consequences rather than leaks. Spend special attention treating on Divine and Perfect Order concerning these plants.

"It will intensify our work in this dimension to redirect the *relocation of specific people* and officiate all responsibilities without directly interfering with the will and destiny of mankind. We bombard with high vibrations and wisdom as helpers through the fourth dimension. The ultimate acceptance or rejection is an individual soul decision.

"Take some time each day to be isolated and know that you are not alone, and listen to those who do surround you then. Allow your bodies to clear all emotional blocks as quickly as your soul is calling you. *The clearer the vehicles, the greater the ability to serve.* Walk quietly, calmly, and beautifully through the world. Golden will be the touch of Love you

106

will bring to others. Golden Love and Light—Lytton, St. Germain, Cassion."

* * *

Johnny Prochaska, a scientist who serves also as spiritual messenger, has spent many years in nuclear research and air pollution. We have a pungent passage from him concerning earth events:

"When major quakes rock Los Angeles and California, they will not completely collapse the state until a major quake down the fault line of the Mississippi River. This midwest quake will give a warning quake and in twelve hours, a second devastating quake will divide the continent. After that, major triggers around the world will occur. First, Los Angeles; then New York, then Italy, etc.

"Solar flare activities will cause hotter heat, sickness and insanity. Do not overexpose yourself to the sun. These solar flares will tilt the axis more and cause climactic changes.

"The last four years there has been a hold up in activities for more internal refinement. Even twenty years ago prayers went out for the final days to be shortened in length and not in winter. They have *now been cut from seven years to one and a half at the most.*

"There may be a *limited* nuclear war initiated by Israel-Arab states. The ark and other valuable spiritual and technical items left in the earth will be lifted by the Space Brothers and returned at reconstruction.

"The orbits of the planets are changing because of the energies of the planets. Solar flares are causing high cosmic radiation which is hitting atoms and smashing them. The changes happening to heavy mineral atoms are causing them to throw off reflections which are even now causing unidentified diseases.

"The combination of earth's energy plus the negative energies is affecting the human aura now, which accounts for much

107

migration to clear open spaces."

* * *

One evening, after dispensing with the required identifications and interdimensional protocol, Munton spoke to me concerning the possible bypass of another solar system:

"In these closing days there is much preparation to be made on spiritual levels. A great manifestation of devotion will sweep across the planet as souls become aware of the actual possibilities that hover in the near future. You have read of a collision of comets. It could be more involved than that. For it is true, there is another solar system which at present is on a straight course for your own position in the atmosphere. This is the true reason for deep concern on the part of such as beloved Soltec and Voltra and astrophysicists here who carefully monitor and register these activities. There is the possibility of a disturbance from the force field of another solar system coming closer each year. It will not need to actually enter your atmosphere to bring reactions within the electromagnetic field of planet Earth. It can be a great distance away, yet nevertheless make its effects penetrable enough to cause much havoc to earth's situation. This fact is another cause for extreme planning on our part for perfect coordination in all evacuation procedures. We are now organized to the extent that *total evacuation could be completed within fifteen minutes of earth time!*

"The approach of another body or system within your magnetic field would be known to us long before your scientific community would be aware of it. There are universal satellites and fact-gathering devices upon them that make those of earth appear as toys. We are prepared for this occurrence completely, along with all other possibilities. I mention this to your readers, in the event that messages concerning this may have reached some and produced fear. This fear is *inadvisable* and *unnecessary,* for those who have lived in love and served the

Light upon the planet, *will not remain to witness any catastrophe:* We send you, rather, the comfort and the assurance that your Heavenly Father knoweth all your needs before they are known to you. This material should be included in the book. I thank you. This is Anton, of the Silver Fleet."

* * *

One of the earlier messages received for this book was one which came while still in Utah—one of great urgency from beloved Soltec concerning coastal changes.

"Good evening, Tuella. This is Soltec speaking once again. I greet you in the Great Light. We have been alerted that another book is in preparation. As Commander of the Great Phoenix, that monitors all scientific situations for this hemisphere, I have been invited to speak with you at an early opportunity whenever the door would be opened for me to do so.

"As you know, we have monitored the planet for many civilizations. We have scanned our records and perused every detail to gather material that might prove of interest to humanity concerning their destiny and the destiny of the planet.

"I have personally monitored the coastlines along the west for many years, as has my father (Monka) before me. Now it would appear that soon the time would come when these labors will prove to be not only vital in all of our undertakings, but important in the saving of many lives. We have organized our forces to such an extent that within one minute of time, or sixty seconds in your time scheme, we can evacuate two-thirds of the western coast should that prove necessary. We have organized our communication system providing for a message to be transmitted to each craft simultaneously. Each Commander and lesser leader is totally prepared to do exactly what they are supposed to do in their assigned area. Therefore we do feel fully prepared and ready for whatever takes place.

"We are not able to give you details and descriptions of what will take place, or exactly when and where. We must confine ourselves to more general expression because so many variables are present. Even if we did know these things, which we do not, it is doubtful that we would be permitted to spread such facts to the population. However, there is a certain sequence of events that can be scientifically and philosophically projected with reasonable success and accuracy.

"For example: It is evident that volcanic action will shortly erupt on the earth crust. We have scientifically determined action within subterranean levels. An unrest within the bowels of the earth has indicated to us that soon many volcanoes will erupt and disturb many areas. This first action will probably come in the Mediterranean area and along the western coastline of America and into Hawaii and that area of the Pacific. There is very little we can do to prevent this action, but we can lessen the depth of the destruction once the eruption has begun. We do have scientific means of deploying such things as will reach within the heart of these eruptions and cool them down. We will be very busy and active in this service.

"The reaction throughout the planet to these outer disturbances will follow very shortly in the wake of these occurrences. This reaction is similar to the domino effect. For one occurrence activates and produces another within subterranean levels of the earth. Therefore, it appears that within a very short time these eruptions will activate earthquakes along the western seaboard through the fault-lines there.

"The possibility is great that some of these earthquake maneuvers will be of great magnitude. We urge the children of Light now to withdraw from the shores in those places, and to penetrate inland as far as their circumstances permit.

"During these western disturbances we further anticipate a series of tidal waves to come to the southern portion of the Atlantic seaboard that will create much chaos and destruction in the Bermuda area, the Caribbean and the coastline of Florida. Again, we urge the children of Light to withdraw upward and inward to the inland and away from the coastline there.

"As Commander of one of the key monitoring spacecraft that patrols the entire hemisphere for the Ashtar Command, it is my duty to keep in closest contact with all incoming data and the newest information. This sequence has been our conclusion as many of us have sat together in the higher councils and looked upon the problems of Terra presently in the making.

"In the eastern sector, the disturbances which are below the surface of the ocean will move northward up the Atlantic coast with pockets of heavy storms for both England and the American seaboard. We urge the persons of Light along these areas also to withdraw inward away from the water and the lash of winds upon them from these vast storms that will be precipitated by the tidal waves that come first.

"As I have patrolled in my ship, the Phoenix, observing the land from the north to the south on both of the coastlines—north in Canada and south into the coast of South America, it has been a great trial to me to realize that these things are already set into motion upon the earth. It is our desire through this messenger to send these words of helpful warning to all now occupying all of the coastlines. The actions of these great bodies of water shall be severe. They will lash upon the lands with no respect of persons or property. On behalf of the Interplanetary Alliance within the Solar System, I, Soltec, urge this hemisphere to heed my words and to be in preparation for such an emergency as I have described.

"There is still time to prepare yourselves as much as possible. There yet is time to relocate yourselves into safer areas and to consider and weigh our words in your consciousness. Consider this, my beloved brethren of earth. If we are wrong, you have lost nothing; but if we are right, you have gained your very lives, and all that you have in this life.

"And so, we can do no more than send forth the words which I have given you, along with our love and blessings, with the hope that you will listen and consider for your own personal sakes, the messages that are now sent to humanity of this

111

hemisphere. I am Commander Soltec, of Spacecraft Phoenix, monitoring your world for the Ashtar Command, in the Authority of Jesus the Christ, Our Beloved Commander, and the Spiritual Hierarchy of this Solar System."

* * *

Immediately upon my arrival back home, I received a telephone call from a close friend, Jeanette M., who passed along a dream. In the dream Jeanette saw a tremendous black cloud of colossal size, heading toward Houston, her home. It was moving inland fast, at great speed. A Being appeared beside her and told her, "This hurricane will smash the Gulf Coast. It is like a great wall that will cover the land. The wind is of such an intense nature that people do not realize it contains a wall of water also." Jeanette was told that where she lives the land would be totally covered with water soon. The Light group there has often diligently worked with impending storms, preventing them from coming in, or redirecting them, but she was told that "in this one, you will not be able to work on it. We will call you. DO NOT FORGET!" Then she awakened. The harmony of this dream with the message of Soltec was most unusual, especially when I considered the fact that both her dream and the message to me *were received within the same twenty-four hour period*—hers in Houston and mine far away in Utah!

In late June, Brother Soltec spoke to a group through the fine messengership of Bob Young, of Showlow, Arizona. In the message given at that time, Soltec confirmed that there would be a polar shift of 14°, with a cooling of 10% at the north pole. He also stated that the eruption of the Mexico volcano would affect the planet for five years, and that the flow of its ash was speeding up the shift. Soltec also explained that the three days of darkness (most of us have wondered about) would accompany the polar shift. It was not my privilege to attend this group meeting, but my information was passed along by a very reliable source, in whom I have absolute confidence.

* * *

When one weighs in the balance all of these contingencies, it is clear that an evacuation of this planet is a certain inevitability!

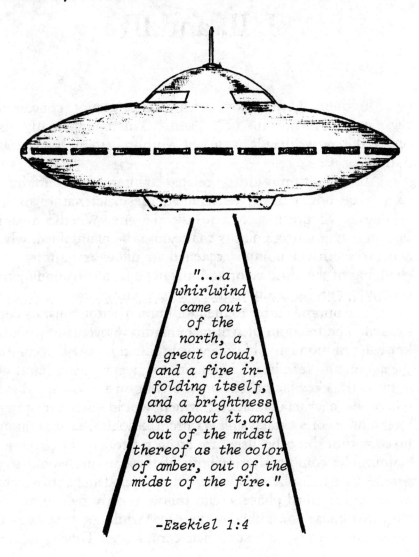

"...a whirlwind came out of the north, a great cloud, and a fire infolding itself, and a brightness was about it, and out of the midst thereof as the color of amber, out of the midst of the fire."

-Ezekiel 1:4

The Great Exodus
I, II, and III

Undoubtedly, the most often asked question concerning these evacuation details is, "When?" This is apparently also one of the most difficult to answer. Kuthumi attempts an explanation for us:

"The situation is greatly related to international affairs. It cannot be dogmatically determined the exact nature of the event that will precipitate these crucial events. Whether a panic button reaction or a polarity that cannot be maintained, when a certain critical point is reached in planetary affairs, the changing of the auric color and magnetic field surrounding the earth will automatically trigger the plan into action.

"The unpredictable element of human action must be considered. The freedom of will of humanity prevents any actual knowing of moment and time when these things will occur, for the action and reaction of humanity to given influences and situations are a key factor. The onset of war on a devastating level would be a crucial incident, which would then precipitate intervention of a cataclysmic nature. Geological factors taking place within the orbit itself are an intricate part of triggering action. The combination of both of these events would trigger the first two phases of evacuation immediately, in a secret manner. The third phase would follow shortly thereafter. For the third phase is a public occurrence, while the first two are covert maneuvers, to insure their completion. Time-wise, it is impossible to yet tell precisely how the nations will go or when they will yield to the crisis situation and blow the world apart. The Legion of Earth-based Commanders will already have had their training and briefing. It is imperative this be completed while there is time."

* * *

I have been told that while basically most of the lift-up will be invisible to others, it will not necessarily be, exclusively, for all three phases. There will be some landings where the people just walk onto the ships. When they cannot land or do not have open areas, then they will resort to other methods. There may be survivors floating in water, from earthquakes, and the land may become jellolike in many places, making the levitation beam a necessary procedure.

Another recurring question is, "Where will the rescued be taken?" Answers that I have received cannot be specific. Destination will depend on age as well as enlightenment level. Some will be put to sleep to lessen the trauma. Some will remain on the ships, depending on their ability to continue in service. Some will be escorted to other planets where acclimation is possible, while others may be transferred to the tremendous city-like ships.

Destination depends on the individual survivor, his life patterns and spiritual evolvement. Some who qualify to be lifted up will be in need of treatment. This will be provided. Others will be on the right level, but will require education and training in areas designed for that purpose. The length of time involved in removal will depend on the nature of what has taken place upon the earth. In some cases where earth devastation is present locally, some may merely be relocated to another area.

Johnnie Prochaska, reader of the Akashic records, has graphically answered the above question. He is quoted here verbatim:

"Much of the domes and dome cities people are visually seeing exist on Uranus. Many evacuees will be sent to there from earth. Many will arrive in suspended animation. Souls will be stepping into already-prepared cloned bodies, while others will transfer their third dimension vehicles to the fourth dimensional ones. Women will have 18-year-old bodies and men, 24 to 25. Any older vehicles will be overhauled.

"When evacuation does occur, there will be several ways of removal. There will not be as much planned boarding as was originally planned. More will go in the raptured type and be gone in a second just before or during a major earth change. In all the confusion, none will suspect. The experiment where this was tried was in a past major quake in China, where 200,000 were secretly removed."

* * *

During the research in Utah in cooperation with Eve Carney, an interesting bit of information came through. After a long pause in the Silence, she suddenly remarked, "One of the astral heavens has been closed! I'm seeing seven astral levels. The door of one has been totally shut off. Whoever is there is certainly going to remain there for awhile. They are there now and will need to remain there another 26,000 year span and then they will be given another opportunity toward evolution. I see that the next astral level is also going to be closed so that the complete cleansing of the planet can be thoroughly accomplished. That second level corresponds to the dark influences and resultant problems. With the sealing off of these two levels, the mission of the Special Volunteers will proceed smoother."

We also discussed at some length with our spiritual teachers the eclipses of 1982. Each eclipse affects the four lower bodies, either pulling them apart or integrating them harmoniously according to the individual soul. One who flows with the Light will get a closer and closer alignment of the four

116

lower bodies. One who is discordant with the Light will become more disrupted in matters of soul integration. The eclipse energies work in this manner.

* * *

There have been scattered and random reports in the past concerning great landings, even *en masse*, of Mother Ships, here and there and yonder. World Teacher Kuthumi has clarified this conjecture and requested that it be included here:

"The Space Confederation has announced that the coming evacuation will not necessarily involve landings except in rare isolated areas. They have measured the hostility factor within the center core of your protective forces, your local and national military stands throughout the planet. It was determined that in most cases, a large majority of these forces would openly attack us and fire upon us in the event of our appearing. This they would do even in disastrous circumstances, and disrupt rescue, thinking it to be some form of invasion.

"We are therefore forced to forsake almost all landings that had been planned and to resort to the invisible levitation plan. This means that those who are calling for our assistance *will need to believe that we are there.* Those with the vision to see us, our ships and those who are being lifted, will be of great benefit to those who do not see. It is still hoped throughout the Confederation that this material will fall into many hands who are a part of these policing groups and military reinforcements, and that this information will gentle the hostile spirit when these events do come to pass. For to openly offer our rescue assistance would be far less complicated than to enter your atmosphere incognito and invisible. Please place this appeal within your text, and trust that it may change the attitude of some who do not understand. I am Kuthumi, speaking for the Alliance for Peace in the Universe. Thank you."

* * *

117

Personally, I have greatly appreciated the words of Commander Jycondria, Assistant to Ashtar, as they have been given to us through spiritual messenger Lyara. Again, we share his words:

"As the scenario reaches its final stages it will be experienced as a great time warp. Time will appear to stand still in some experiences and in others, to feel like entire lifetimes in hours, moments, or days. If you waste your precious energy in reflecting upon the past, it will only further confuse the mental body, which has no references but previous earth tapes, and cause more tension and anxiety in the emotional body. To live in anticipation of tomorrow and the days to come is equally unfair, because as always, the preparations, understanding, and endurance *will be given when you need it!*

"Some of you are now being given foresight or foreknowledge. It is appropriate as a preparation and conditioning, so that you are given both understanding and emotional growth processes to *soften the shock* and be more effective to share your processes with others during actual impact times. Much of this preparation is unconscious and for some, conscious. Each of you will be experiencing a magnification of unresolved energies now—through the physical, emotional vehicles for complete release."

Phase I

PHASE I of the Great Exodus of souls from the planet will take place at a moment's notice when it is determined that the inhabitants are in danger. The very second the great computers show that needle has gone across a certain point, every satellite and participating craft, already in readiness, will swing into action. If it is not global in nature, but local areas of great danger, persons may be lifted only until the danger subsides and just as suddenly returned without recall. (In the former gatherings of the Earthean Eagles, most all will be permitted recall, being of a spiritual nature that permits it). The decisive events

118

that trigger Phase I depend upon man and his actions and activities.

PHASE I of the global evacuation will come as the twinkling of an eye, with no time for any pre-warning of any significance. It will be a secret taking away of spiritual leaders and teachers of the Light workers, but *not those of the Special Legion* who will remain until the last phase is completed. Phase I participants will be momentarily alerted at the time of any threat to the planet or its crust. Some may be notified where to go and when. In this covert rescue they will be invisibly levitated by beam to smaller ships that wait, on which they will be transported to the great mother ships anchored high in the atmosphere. Again it was repeated for emphasis, Phase I will remove all of the Earth Volunteers on assignment except those of the Special Legion who remain, highly protected, till all evacuation is completed.

It was stressed that it was impossible for them to state or give a figure of how many will participate in any of the removals because of the constant fluctuating population of the planet through death or intervention of human will, and the opening of the chakras of the new ones.

As mentioned earlier, there will be *no landing areas* for Phase I. They will be overhead and none will land. The scout ships will come wherever these special persons are.

Phase II

Our Space Friends have explained that the second phase of the global evacuation are those who have followed the Leaders and Teachers of Light, and the children! This second phase will be as close to the first as time permits, with the second immediately following the first. The second phase is vital, as we return for the children of all ages and races. The child does not have the power of choice in understanding nor personal accountability. (Note: See the message of Arcturus, page 108, in WORLD MESSAGES FOR THE COMING DECADE).

119

In Jycondria's continuing message through Lyara, he also speaks of the children:

"The children will naturally be lifted before the final phase of evacuation. Some of you will assist young souls of children and will be instruments in both entertainment and love until they are safely removed. Many will move up with them during evacuation so that they may pass up with the least amount of trauma possible.

"Naturally most children will be boarded asleep—suspended animation—for the trauma of events would be too strenuous until they are to be awakened. The children will be initiated also, and as their veils are lifted, they will appear as wise, mature adults in young bodies with very worthy assignments of service and education like the rest of you. Nurturing assignments which you as parents have received will be ended, as you rejoice in the graduation and beauty of these souls. Through the unlimited application of love, you will always be able to communicate with others. Telepathy, television, and teleportation will be among your unlimited abilities that you are awakening to. Be not concerned about the children, for they will be lovingly provided for."

Andromeda Rex has also given me these comforting words:

"In this phase the children will be attended to first, and special great ships of paramount love vibration are especially prepared, with those of great love to be in attendance upon these children. Your children will not be lost from you. There are tracers within our complicated equipment which can locate every soul. You can request and will be given this information to comfort your hearts while you tarry with us."

* * *

Captain Avalon has added this bit of information to the whole:

"There has been discussion of relocating medical person-

120

nel. This is an emergency contingency that is not necessarily a part of global evacuation. In times of great stress and truly phenomenal needs in a certain area, that is not a threat to the planet, then those members of the Special Legion who do have the necessary vocational attributes will agree to be approached in emergencies for these relocations.

"If only a portion of the planet or certain sections are in danger or peril, a mass of persons may be relocated to another safer area. This would not constitute sufficient reason for evacuation, but mercy would permit a relocation for them. In that case, expertise and abilities of the Special Volunteers would accompany them to organize and care for them. Our ships are assigned to pick up persons of specific groupings. Those assigned to medical personnel would disperse them and supplies to the neediest areas of the planet, for the needs throughout the planet will be diversified, and the ability to meet those needs must be balanced. Thus, much of the lifting of these medically trained persons will be for relocating them where great need is present. This kind of emergency action would fall into the activities of Phase II. There could be much reshuffling of masses of persons to areas safer, cooler, warmer, drier, or whatever is vital at that moment of time, yet not threatening planetary annihilation."

Phase III

Enoch prophesied the returning Lord would have an entourage of at least ten thousand saints (Jude 14), but from the information we now have, that figure could be updated to many millions. Various Commanders of the Ashtar Command have explained to me that in whatever time remains, the sky will be filled with ships extending an invitation to rescue whosoever is without fear and whose vibratory frequency is sufficient to bear the levitation beams. Due to the planetary turbulence at the time, there will be only limited landings for this mass evacuation. This final removal takes place as time permits and in accordance with whatever disaster is prevalent.

"This will be a mass hovering in the skies for whoever is unafraid to join with us to be rescued. The *ultimate destination of these will be determined later.* The moment at hand will require only that they be without fear and of sufficient vibratory frequency to withstand the levitating beam around them. Phase III makes up the invitation to the multitudes to welcome whomsoever can withstand the activities of rescue and accept our call, in whatever few moments are left, for we cannot linger in your atmosphere when the turbulence gets underway. This final lift-off will, of course, also include those faithful Earth Commanders who have borne the heavy responsibility of earth details in preparation for our coming. These are the kinds of things that will be discussed with them at their briefings in the secret councils."

* * *

Important instruction from Lytton through Lyara should be included here:

"Energies must be totally cohesed in the moment of each day, with a total commitment to the energies. Many are now called for the magnitude of work to transpire. Few will be *ready* for this committed level of service. The wheat *is* being separated from the chaff. Each Light Worker will be given multiple hats —roles of service—as they have been given multiple talents. It is most important in maintaining balance with these responsibilities to separate your energies from yesterdays or tomorrows or anything unrelated to each exact moment and project. Then, as the Holy Spirit descends upon you, perfect direction and action will transpire with phenomenal and unprecedented levels of service.

"Put your quiet moments and spiritual growth as number I. Be not attached to planetary service. Only some will be facilitated and they will be the combined efforts of many toward rapid necessary projects. The *major projects* of the evolution of mankind at a consciousness level will not occur until the inter-ruption of life on the planet. Then both those who exit on the ships and those who drop their vehicles will be taken into vari-ous schools and experiences for their growth."

* * *

More informative and helpful details make up the conclu-sion of Commander Jycondria's message shared by Lyara:

"Some of you are to be gatherers of supplies and essentials for others that will come to you in the final moments ahead. Simplify your lives that you will not be burdened with extrane-ous material possessions. Many of your homes will become filled *with your spiritual family* before departure, and space will become a premium.

"Besides the citizens of earth, successful evacuation will be given to all the spiritual centers both in the etheric and the physical in the mountains and beneath the earth. Records, energy and healing devices, and all instruments of Brother-hoods, will be removed to be returned with life on earth at a later day. Even today's plants and animal specimens (similar to the enactment of Noah's ark) are being removed to various planets for successful hybridization to vibrationally prepare for their return. Nature spirits and plant and animal devas are being removed to continue their evolution and return in greater forms and expressions. Ships which have been left within the earth for this time *will be reactivated,* as they will be *locally used* and then lifted with the evacuation. The civilizations within middle earth *which serve the Light* will be evacuated as well as all life upon the surface. No life will be left for the cleansing cycle, in any dimension or expression.

"You have been previously instructed as to the "why's"—now you have received more instructions as to the "how's." Trust the perfection, preciseness and experience of the Inter-galactic Fleet. Many contingencies and details which you could not even fathom at this time have been allowed for. Remain calm, trust the process, and all will go smoothly with lift-off. We are not only manifesting the lights in the sky, but expanding the love and understanding in your heart. Trust our words! Our actions will speak for themselves. Welcome home. The reunion will soon be occurring aboard the ships. Bless you."— Jycondria (Assistant to Ashtar).

* * *

In response to some questions asked of my Space Friends, I was told that the areas of earth to be repopulated first will depend totally upon what nature of cataclysm has taken place upon the planet. Some members of the Intergalactic Fleet will relocate with us for assistance in rehabilitating the survivors and introducing helpful advances to the planet, as advisors in many fields such as education, art, government, horticulture, and spiritual guidance.

Voltra, a leading Space Psychologist with the Commands, spoke to me of these blessings:

"I command a fleet of those who monitor the vibratory rate of mankind, as well as the frequency changes in nature and all manifest life upon the planet. It is a great joy to us when the data banks fill with good tidings of another soul, here and there, who has turned to the unfolding Light and awakened to truth in accordance with his own understanding of things. Such a soul, if it continues to seek, will ultimately find the uninhibited truth of all things and add his or her measure of Light to that already upon the planet.

"We have so much scientific data to share with earth, and much benevolent knowledge to give you for your own well-being and blessing, but these must be withheld until that time when hu-man has evolved into Man and can be invested with great revelations. You will see many things upon our ships that will astound you and truly electrify your understanding of the Laws of the Universe.

"There is so much that you do not understand and upon

124

which you are building false conclusions. Your concepts of gravity and energy are cause for much error in your approach to applied physics. The coming interplanetary fellowship will bring men of earth unheard scientific enlightenment, under the new order. Already many of those who will be given these formulas and concepts are born unto you and bring with them the capability of understanding new principles. These new thoughts will truly bring in a Golden Age of enlightenment and abundance.

"When war is removed from your plane of existence and love prevails upon earth, then all of the great blessings of other worlds will be shared freely with you in perfect love. Fret not for the changes that must come to make this possible. Think only the great new earth to come with deliverance, health and peace. I am Voltra, who speaks in the brightness of Our Radiant One. Vasu, Vasu. I am Voltra."

Xyletron, of the Intergalactic Fleet, speaking through Lyara, puts it bluntly:

"Earth—as a playground and educational institution—is *CLOSING DOWN FOR A PERIOD*. After a cleansing and remodeling has transpired, it will be reopened, but with a greater curriculum and staff to challenge the eager students of life into more preparations for even greater horizons that will challenge them after graduation. After successful preparations, those returning to earth will know the laws and be prepared to live in harmony with them."

* * *

Lyara also shares these words from our Beloved Jesus:

"You are rapidly moving internally from an awareness of a possibility of these events to pass on to an absolute knowing that the accounting and recording must be activated now. The trumpets will be soon sounded, and with the sounding, will come forth my children to be lifted up by the vibration each of your souls have achieved. Commitment to an institution, church, or synagogue will not assure salvation. Only those who have sincerely sought out the love of God in their hearts and then applied those higher principles of service and joy toward the higher development and service to others. Knowledge from booklearning will profit nothing. The gathering of knowledge and wisdom in thought and deed will count for everything.

"Woe, that I weep for the children who have not learned from earth and will not be prepared to move into the higher worlds with me. They must suffer more experiences until they surrender to the loving Father who can cleanse their pain, dry their tears, and purify their hearts. Many are called, as always, but few have developed the eyes to see and the ears to hear.

"Let go immediately of any unresolved energies or emotions which are binding you to earth, whether it is the sin of attachment to material possessions or the continual lustful thoughts of passion in your mind. Release your resentments, your fears, your needs to feed your ego. Forgive your neighbor, your friends, and even the bums in your community. Judge nothing as less than Divine, perfect in its own unique way. Accept everything equally as beautiful and good. Trust that life force/ source to sustain you with all that you need now and in the days to come. All is God! Awaken to the glory of that joy as creation is spun from the illusion of separation into the Oneness of creation for all to witness that participate.

"Oh, Father, bless and rejoice for each soul that moves forward with me. Bless those who are not ready, that their evolution be quickened.

"My love constantly abides with all of you. Soon you will see me, as now you consciously feel me."—Jesus

The designers of this volume have asked that I repeat a message that came some time earlier this year from the great Chohan, Hilarion. The message has already appeared in print in several places, but it is an appeal that is vital and bears repeating once again:

"I am Hilarion, thy Brother of the Emerald Ray. I have

126

returned to you once again in order that my words might be broadcast to the people who serve the Light and the manifesto of the Ascended Masters who guard and guide the planet Earth.

"IT IS IMPERATIVE THAT NOW AT THIS TIME THE PERSONS WHO ARE CONNECTED IN ANY WAY WITH THE REPRESENTATION OF THE SPIRITUAL HIERARCHY SHALL BEGIN TO COME TOGETHER IN ONENESS AND IN LOVE AND TOLERANCE OF ONE ANOTHER, IN ORDER THAT A GREAT PINK CLOUD OF LOVE AND UNITY MIGHT FLOAT THROUGHOUT THE LAND AND BRING BLESSING TO ITS PEOPLE. WE LOOK UPON MANY DIVISIONS AND MANY VARIATIONS OF THE GREAT TRUTH, BUT WE SEE WITHIN ALL AND THROUGH ALL, A GREAT LACK OF COHESION AND INNER ONENESS DESIGNED TOWARD A BRINGING TOGETHER OF THE SOULS WHO SERVE UNDER MANY BANNERS. I SPEAK TO YOU NOW, MY BELOVED ONES, OF THE NEW AGE UNDERSTANDING. I SPEAK TO THOSE WHO ARE THE ENLIGHTENED ONES. I SPEAK TO THOSE WHO HAVE FOUND THEIR WAY OUT FROM THE COALITIONS OF DARKNESS AND MANMADE HIERARCHIES OF BONDAGE. I SPEAK TO OUR SONS AND DAUGHTERS OF WISDOM AND DELIVERANCE. I CALL FOR A UNITING OF ALL THOSE LIGHT BEINGS IN WHATEVER RAY OF SERVICE YOU FIND YOURSELVES, IN WHATEVER ALLEGIANCE TO WHATEVER MASTER OR BODY OF REVELATION YOU SERVE IN THE LEGIONS OF LIGHT.

"I CALL FOR A SETTING ASIDE OF ALL ATTITUDES OF SEPARATENESS WITHIN THE FOLD OF OUR EMISSARIES, TO UNITE YOURSELF AS A GREAT IMPENETRABLE WALL OF LIGHT AGAINST THE STRONGHOLDS OF INVASION FROM THE DARK EMISSARIES WHO WOULD SEEING TO DIVIDE YOU AND TO CONQUER YOUR GREAT LIGHT. TAKE CARE

THAT NOT ONE IOTA OF INTERFERENCE FROM THESE SHALL BE PERMITTED NOR TOLERATED WITHIN THY FOLD. HOLD FAST TO A STRONGHOLD OF BLUE LIGHT AROUND EVERY GROUP, EVERY CIRCLE, EVERY EFFORT EXTENDED TOWARD THE ONGOING ENLIGHTENMENT OF THIS DAY. LET NOT ANY DIVISION BE FOUND AMONG YOU, LET NOT THE IMPERFECTIONS OF HUMAN MANIFESTATION DISTURB YOUR INNER PEACE OR YOUR GREAT STILLNESS WITHIN. THROUGH THESE MEANS MUCH GAIN IS LOST, MUCH VICTORY IS WEAKENED BY THE INTERNAL STRIFE OF THE PERSONALITY!

"THIS IS THAT HOUR WHEN THE GREATEST OF LOVE MUST PREVAIL. THE PATIENCE OF LOVE MUST OVERSHADOW EVERY JOINT UNDERTAKING AND EVERY COMBINED EFFORT FOR OUR GREAT HIERARCHAL PROGRAM. CLEANSE YOURSELVES OF ALL HUMAN PETTINESS AND LESSER EMOTIONS THAT FRUSTRATE THE ACTION OF LOVE IN YOUR MIDST. THE TIME IS COME WHEN LOVE MUST UNITE YOU IN ONE SOLIDIFIED NUCLEUS OF PURITY. THE GATES OF HELL ITSELF CANNOT PREVAIL AGAINST LOVE IN UNITED ACTION WITHIN THE BODY OF OUR LIGHTED ONES.

"MY BLESSING AND MY BENEDICTION BE UPON EACH AND EVERY ONE OF YOU WHO SERVE THE GREAT LIGHT IN THIS DAY. THE LIGHT OF GOD SHALL NOT FAIL. I AM HILARION, OF THE EMERALD RAY."

* * *

Andromeda Rex, whom we have come to love so very dearly, brought me this final message as the book neared the closing:

"The Great Evacuation will come upon the world very

suddenly. The flash of emergency events will be as the lightning that flashes in the sky. So sudden and so quick in its happening that it is over almost before you are aware of its presence. And so it will be when the events that warrant this action have come to the planet. It is not possible to totally describe these events, but it is possible to instill at this time into the hearts of humanity the hope and the knowledge of our vigilance and emergency actions on their behalf.

"Our rescue ships will be able to come in close enough in the twinkling of an eye to set the lifting beams in operation in a moment. And all over the globe where events warrant it, this will be the method of evacuation. Mankind will be lifted, levitated shall we say, by the beams from our smaller ships. These smaller craft will in turn taxi the persons to the larger ships overhead, higher in the atmosphere, where there is ample space and quarters and supplies for millions of people.

"It has been explained to you in the past that there is a certain amount of preparedness necessary because of exposure to this powerful beam which will be operating in these circumstances. The frequency of it will be higher than most of your known electrical earthly exposures. Those of extreme density and extreme selfish dispositions—especially at the expense of others—or causing suffering to others, will find extreme physical difficulty in surviving in the frequency of our beams. This is why our messages have been broadcast to mankind over the centuries to lift his own emanations and vibrations to a status of love and selflessness so that in so doing, a compatibility of force-fields will make his rescue possible. Those who have lived closely aligned to the Father's will in their lives and have let the love of the Father flow through them, will have no problem with the frequency of the evacuation rays. For a high state of love in the human heart reacts upon the human force-field surrounding the physical form, giving it an electrical sheath of protection and a blending with the incoming vibrations between now and that time. Indeed, *if enough souls could experience perfect love, there could very well be no need for a removal of humanity.*

"There is nothing to be feared in coming into our midst. We are loving, normal persons, as yourselves, with the attitude of good neighbors and helpers in a time of crisis. We are prepared with clothing, and your foods, and the needs to which you have accustomed yourselves. We will not be guards, but friends, and you will enjoy your time with us, especially as you look upon your planet in its turmoil. Those beamed up in physical form will be accelerated and quickened within that physical form to a more spiritual essence within the body, into what has been termed 'Light' bodies. The physical form will remain the same in appearance to most, but that higher blending of the etheric with the physical will bring about change, and eliminate sickness and physical disharmony among you. There will be a period of time to be spent with us, for your beautiful earth must be healed in its cleansing, and given time to return to its true glory. Then those who have been lifted in the body will be returned to reconstruct a New World and a New Order of things. As you tarry with us, you will be given the opportunity to attend classes and training for the work which will need to be done. You will be given our constant help in doing this; our advice and our technology will be at the disposal of these returning ones. Many others who have been lifted through natural transition will be returned in new bodies to participate in the new awakening. Those who could not participate in the lifting off rescue will be transported, following their natural transition, to locations with a vibration and frequency equal to their own, where they may grow and learn at a pace slower than the new vibration of planet earth. For the earth will be in an accelerated and very high frequency as it finds expression in the Aquarian Age.

"In the beginning of this great occurrence, time will be of the essence and all must be done in great haste and in a minimum of time. We will not have time to tarry, but must work

130

speedily in the phase III portion of the rescue of the multitudes who consciously choose to be included. You must understand that this great activity will only be set into motion when events on earth have reached a crisis. We may not interfere with your lives in any way unnecessarily or too soon. But only in that last moment of danger to the masses will the final stages of evacuation be set into motion. The other two phases will have been completed. The Light Workers, along with those who have followed them and assisted them will already have been removed. The final lift-up will be of the multitudes who desire to come and can participate in time. This phase will continue as long as the situation allows, *WHICH AT BEST, WILL BE BRIEF!*

"Most of you, while in the sleep state, have already been brought into our craft for acclimation and adjustment, the memory of which will be quickened within you as a recall when the true lift-up takes place.

"There is nothing to fear. Let great joy abound in thankfulness to the Father of all, that not one thoughtful detail will be over looked to overshadow you with His Love and His care for you who have put your trust in Him.

"I am Andromeda Rex, one who speaks for the Ashtar Command."

"Thank you, Andromeda!"

* * *

I have chosen to give beloved Matton the last word because of the nature of his appeal. Matton is the busy coordinator of all the volunteer units serving within earth's atmosphere in these final events. He often speaks of the beautiful and loyal dedication to this mission of international and world peace, of these men and women of other worlds who serve here. His desire with this message was to speak of the coming armadas of craft in the final stage of evacuation.

"The hour when the call is extended to mankind, while very broad and universal, will come very quickly and will not

131

be extended but for a very short period of time. At that point in time, the atmosphere will be dangerous to us as well as to you earthlings, and to linger in it would destroy us both. Therefore, let me stress that humankind cannot wait until that moment to decide what they will do, for the *time will be so limited* and those who choose first will be taken first. It would be well for mankind *to think on these things now,* and ask himself what he will do in that eventuality. Not only that, but to ask himself also whether or not he would qualify for survival of the operation, in terms of personal frequencies and attitudes. There will be no time then to set about changing oneself, or beginning then to attempt personal change within one's lower bodies. What a man is within himself will be revealed by all to see when he steps into those levitation rays. Density and low vibrations will not survive them, only the higher aspired mind and the pure heart will be immune to them.

"Now it is an incredible thing to us that earth persons would so long neglect that which is the *only reality* of all life. It is not the materialistic accumulations of a lifetime that matter at all in the hour when you face your rescue. Human opinions and the perils of pride, the falsity of ego-centered thought and activity, will all perish in the twinkling of an eye. Only love for others will make the ascension, service to others will lay up treasures in heaven, but *selfishness and guile* will be destroyed in that hour.

"Therefore, we plead with all souls *NOW,* to think on these things, to consider the innermost parts of being, and judge yourselves that ye be not judged, and receive the help of the incoming great rays now being poured upon the planet. These great rays are here to assist you in your spiritual aspirations and if that is the desire of your heart, you have much heavenly assistance coming to you at this time. Now is the time to make yourself ready to be taken by the ships. Not to sit in the seat of the scornful, but to wholeheartedly enter into the spirit of love for those who come and desire even now to begin to speak to others of this great plan to come. At least those of your immediate family and immediate circle of friends. Think on these things together. Think of the vibrational compatibility that is necessary to be with us, to live with us, until your earth home is prepared for you once again. I plead with you, *ponder* these things. This book is released now, for the small portion of time that remains, that humanity would still have an opportunity to return to the blessed life and the guidance of the guardians to take you safely home.

"How will you feel within your own being when your eyes behold the sky black with craft over your head? How will you feel? Thankful? Frightened? Inadequate? Insecure? Or rejoicing and eager to be taken out of the turmoil. This final massive maneuver of Phase III will be humanity's last opportunity to retain the present physical form and be kept within our ships until the calamities be passed.

This is Matton, closing the contact. Thank you, Tuella."

* * *

"And my heartfelt thanks to each and every one of you, Dear Brothers, for this wonderful opportunity to serve with you.

This is Tuella…closing the book!"

Epilogue

By the Dawn's Early Light...

The compilation was nearing completion. Necessary housework haunted me. Friends were thinking I had withdrawn from the human race! Dinner invitations went begging. My public life had almost ceased. During these busy days, while attempting to meet a publishing deadline given by my Space Friends, I had been arising about an hour before sunrise, when first light appeared in the eastern sky.

One morning as I turned to silence the alarm, my gaze fell on the eastern bedroom window. There, beyond the left corner, I beheld *the largest, most brilliant ship I had ever seen*. A long groan escaped as I thrilled with peace and love, watching it beautify the clear and otherwise empty sky. Stars were no longer visible. Much light had already spread across the horizon. The edge of the magnificent craft sparkled as if rimmed in diamonds strategically spaced at certain points. The distance was great; nevertheless, I realized its tremendous size, and thought surely this must be one of those etheric cities they speak of.

My window is five feet wide, but two feet are obscured by drapes. In the remaining viewing area, I watched this stately craft majestically move very slowly in a diagonal path toward the upper right hand corner area of my observation point. With great joy and amazement, I carefully observed as its slow-moving brilliance silently disappeared behind a nearby telephone pole and then gradually slipped out beyond the other side. Again, I traced its sparkling points as they hid, one by

135

one, behind the leafy limbs of a small tree, to reappear within my vision beyond each limb. While my eyes were fixed upon the awesome wonder of it all, on the ceiling just above the window a sparkling flash of light exploded, and in a second, was gone again. I wanted to phone a nearby friend, but I was rooted to the spot.

It's deliberate, easy pace across the sky seemed to be saying, *"Hey.' Look us over!"* In fact, it moved so slowly that had I not been taking position marks by the panes of the window and the nearby telephone pole in its relationship to the little tree, I might have missed its movement. At first observance, I ran to the east end of the house for a better look, but found the ship to be totally obscured by the mulberry trees. I flew back to my observation window, and it was then I discovered it had moved from my former position marks. I decided to watch it intently, in position with the pole, and discovered the slow, steady, easterly upward movement. To a casual passerby just glancing at the sky, movement would have been unnoticeable.

As the great ship gradually climbed higher and traveled into the east away from me, it became smaller and smaller in appearance until it remained only about one-fifth its first appearance in diameter. I had been too enraptured by the scene to attempt communication, but as I relaxed in the moments following, I was told they would appear each morning at six. I began to wonder if the incident was related to their book. It had first appeared low and large at about 5:45 a.m. and had taken forty minutes to negotiate diagonally the observation area up and across my window. I was determined to be ready the next morning with camera, binoculars, tape recorder, and notebook. Better still, I would be outside at the property's east end by 5:00 a.m.!

For hours afterwards I could not discipline my mind to remain long on anything else. My eyes filled with tears again and again. It was as if they were saying, *"We want YOU to see and know that we are real, that we ARE here...and then...*

136

TELL THEM." I knew I should write down the date and the time. When I consulted the calendar, I had another shock. The date was a private anniversary between my Space Friends and me. Exactly two years ago this date—August 27—began the vigil for receiving the twenty-seven dictations for WORLD MESSAGES FOR THE COMING DECADE, and it was on that date in the evening very late that I had seen my only other star ship like this one! It filled me with much comfort to consider they might be remembering also, and celebrating with me in this way, but that was pure conjecture. It made its appearance low on the horizon above the southernmost tip of Cook mountains, and I supposed it had come out of them.

At 11:30 a.m. the overhead electric light in my dark study blinked three times, quickly, but the other lights did not. I entered the alert.

"*Tuella, this is Anton, of the Silver Fleet at Cook mountain headquarters. I am interrupting your day to bring you this information. The ship that you saw this morning is the one on which this sector Gathering will take place and the one into which evacuees will be brought. It was much farther away than you think. It was far beyond the end of our mountains. It is the same ship which positioned above you two years ago and it is a city-size ship, being almost one hundred miles in diameter. Your mind cannot grasp the significance of these dimensions (mentally, I quickly agreed). The ship has come to remain in this general area throughout October. It has Andromeda Rex and Ashtar both aboard, and it will appear THREE TIMES AS A SIGN. Watch for it each morning faithfully, and they will respond to your love and appear.*

"*Though you have received a beam from it earlier, the beam was strengthened this morning as you gazed upon it. I have felt the necessity to intrude to give you these answers, understanding how curious you are concerning the appearance. The ship did NOT come up out of our installation here. It is MUCH too large to be based here. This ship does not land, but remains in a cruise pattern. Its appearance IS related to our book. As it departed, it did not leave your sector, but positioned itself in the higher atmosphere. You were permitted to see it for reasons that will be shared by them soon."*

That evening at my regular 9:00 p.m. appointment with them, Andromeda Rex was the first to speak:

"Greetings in the Light of Our Beloved. I am speaking to you directly form the Command Ship you saw this morning. We have permitted you this experience for specific reasons. We will appear to you two more times when the skies are clear, to seal the vision and to complete the testimony for others. Then the sightings will end. This is the purpose and the confirmation, as well as for your own infilling of faith and confidence. You cannot convince them if the trumpet gives an uncertain sound. You must see and be convinced beyond any shadow of a doubt that the words we speak are true and your experience is real. This experience will soften and humanize the impact of the messages we have sent like a final exclamation point. We request that you write this account to be shared at the close of the book, to linger in the memory of the readers.

"Be posted at dawn for the next several days until the three sightings are fulfilled. Then they will be concluded. I am Andromeda, and it is I who will speak at the dawn vigil with a brief message to the people. I am the Commander responsible for this western sector, sharing my mission with Monka, who will oversee the central sector, and Alphon, who heads up the leadership for the eastern sector. Communication was withheld this morning to allow the emotional impact upon your being to have its full sway for that moment. Whenever the eyes are closed, you may recapture, visualize and completely relive that intense moment when you followed our path across the eastern sky."

The following morning I was stationed in my car by 5:00 a.m. I parked at the eastern edge of the farm, away from all structures, for good observation. A dense cloud cover lingered listlessly across the east, without the slightest breeze to encourage its departure. Any sighting was impossible under these conditions. They had specified "clear morning."

On Sunday morning which followed, I turned off the alarm at 5:00, but from extreme overtiredness, it took twenty minutes to maneuver myself into a sitting-up posture. I regretted the delay immediately. The Star Ship was already at "half-window" position. *It was early!* Perhaps because of the dense black cloud rift that covered the upper half of the eastern heaven.

I bounded out the screen door and leaned motionless against the car. I chose a distant telephone pole as a marker to track its movement. The illuminated edge points of its outline were still discernible. Very slowly, it resolutely closed the gap left of the pole, as I remained unmoving in my observation. In its ascension it was taking on the appearance of a star. In fixed pace, it finally disappeared behind the pole. As I watched for its gleam to slide into view on the right side of the pole, the lower edge of the black cloud density touched that point on the pole, and I didn't see it again. Nevertheless, I experienced great joy because they had *kept the promise* to appear twice again. One more to go!

The next dawn I awakened long before the alarm was to sound. By then I was settled into my vigil amid the clutter of recorder, camera, binoculars and notebook. The sky was clear. The stars overhead gleamed like diamonds in a jewel case. It was still too dark to select position markers. I waited. I knew, *with an inner knowing,* this would be the final morning of my vigil. I knew they would come, and I *knew* there would be a final word. Not for me...but for those who would read their book.

For a considerable time I slumped in the car seat, leaning against the door...just waiting. Low on the very horizon line I noticed a very bright light. I assumed it was a street light of yonder Deming. Then, on second thought, I decided to get out of the car to be certain. Focusing the light in my inadequate binoculars, I realized with a start, it was not a street light, for it was already arisen above the horizon line. Its size and its glow compared to the city limits at my lower right. *They had come! They had kept their word!* This was the third appearance, in the trinity of completion, the law of the triangle. I immediately greeted them in my mind, hoping they might courteously blink the lights or something spectacular, but nothing happened. I focused the beautiful ship between two tall stalks of a yucca plant, and waited. They held to the location for about ten minutes, then slowly began to slip away to the right of my vision barricade. The time was 5:58.

I wondered why the yucca plant stood so motionless, and the fenceposts remained so indifferent. Couldn't they hear the pounding of my heart? Why didn't the rocks cry out? Why didn't the Earth tremble as I did? The promised sunrise was spreading a strip of deep peach tones across the horizon. A low elongated cloud was absorbing hues of yellow, as the dawn silently invaded the slumbering desert scene. The great ship had now ascended the length of a "telephone pole" above the pole. I had traced its pathway between the yucca stalks, across three fenceposts, toward a distant telephone pole. In this awe-inspiring moment I had followed its climb through the telephone wires to the cross bars of the pole. I waited in peaceful confidence, knowing it would appear beyond each crossbar at the top of the pole, to adorn the uppermost tip like a jewel atop a royal scepter.

I was warmed within my being, when according to his promise, Andromeda presented his credentials and spoke, while I was locked into a great love vibration:

"WE HAVE COME TO YOU IN THE FATHER'S NAME AND IN HIS LOVE. THIS SIGN IN THE HEAVENS WHICH WE HAVE GIVEN OUR MESSENGER IS A SIGN TO MANKIND THAT OUR WORDS ARE TRUE. THIS VISITATION COMES, THAT OUR WORDS WILL HAVE

IMPACT, FOR THIS IS THE WITNESS TO ALL THAT WE ARE PRESENT WITH YOU. THIS IS THE VITAL MEANING OF OUR MORNING RUNS ACROSS THE EASTERN SKY. IT IS THE FINAL MESSAGE AND THE LAST ACT BEFORE THE CURTAIN IS DRAWN UPON THIS, ANOTHER EFFORT OF THE SPACE ALLIANCE TO CONVINCE MANKIND.

"WE ARE YOUR BROTHERS AND SISTERS FROM OTHER WORLDS AND MEMBERS OF THE ASHTAR COMMAND. PEACE AND BLESSINGS BE YOURS, AND THE LOVE OF THE MOST HIGH LORD GOD OF HOSTS BE UPON ALL OF YOU."

Then slowly, it escaped! Totally free from markers of any kind or any earthly thing, it escaped high into the clear blue of the morning sky. Its movement still appeared to be incredibly slow, and while its appearance diminished in size as it pulled away to the east, its brilliance in my little binoculars continued to thrill the very soul of me. In my thought world, I projected to that time when we of this world would be on and in that Great City, that Great Shining White City, that pulled away from me after its third visitation. A sense of peace settled around me and within me, beyond anything I have ever experienced.

The sun had not yet arisen, but the great light beginning to fill the sky heralded its coming. I wondered if others had watched this brilliant "star" that continued to shine so long after all others had yielded to the advancing dawn. It had now become very small in the distance, and I felt that a part of me had gone with it. Finally, my little opera glasses could scarcely retain the pinpoint of light, and the tears didn't help, but I watched until it dissolved into the etheric.

"Goodbye, dear friends...thank you for coming. I promise...to TELL THEM!"

Then, into the cathedral dome of heaven, above the glowing footlights of nature, came the bursting beauty of a grand finale, as the golden sun arose before me! I watched in mute inspiration this exquisite symbology:

...OF A NEW DAWN FOR HUMANITY; A NEW EXPERIENCE FOR THE BEAUTIFUL EARTH; A NEW DAY FOR MANKIND!

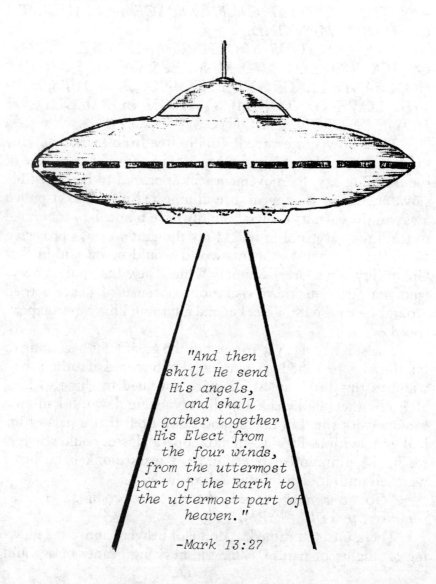

"And then shall He send His angels, and shall gather together His Elect from the four winds, from the uttermost part of the Earth to the uttermost part of heaven."

-Mark 13:27

Appendix

Visions of UFOs in the Last Days

by Timothy Green Beckley

Since the original, privately published, edition of *Project World Evacuation* was released, many readers have come forth with their own visions of the "End Times" to help verify Tuella's most vital messages.

• • •

When UFOs were first seen canvassing the heavens back in the late 1940's, many people thought our planet was being invaded by aliens from outer space. Our concept of otherworldly visitors as flesh eating, slave masters, was fostered by low-budget science-fiction thrillers that always portrayed the occupants of flying saucers in very negative ways. Many remembered the *War of the Worlds* radio broadcast that had our depression-era planet being taken over by Martians with devastating weapons.

With all these very scary impressions floating around in our mind, it's no wonder that the mere thought of ET's landing in our back yard was enough to send us running to the nearest fallout shelter.

Yet, in actuality, based upon an evaluation of all the evidence, it would seem that the majority of UFOnauts mean us no harm. If anything, in a good percentage of cases they appear genuinely interested in our well-being, even going so far as to heal some of those they have communicated with—including poor eyesight and paralysis. There is even one case I know of from South America where an elderly UFO witness grew in a third set of teeth following a close encounter. There are even a hundred or more cases in which actual communications have been established and the aliens warn that we should mend our ways, and give up our war-like behavior before we blow ourselves into ashes. Far from monsters, these beings are usually described as humanoid in appearance, with a super intelligence and a spirituality that far overshadows our puny acceptance of God's laws. Apparently, these beings have followed our Earthly religions since its inception and accept the concept of a universal creator and acknowledge Christ as our savior and protector. Yet despite the overwhelming evidence that many of these accounts are legitimate, there is an apparently organized attempt to keep the true nature of the UFO phenomena from the public. Those in authority and power refuse to acknowledge the existence of UFOs or the "Space Brothers," as these benevolent ETs have come to be identified.

In the months just past, several outspoken ministers have pronounced their belief in UFOs and things non-worldly. Famed evangelist Rev. Billy Graham can be counted among those coming forth. In his book *Angels: God's Secret Agents*, he makes the statement that UFOs "bear striking resemblance to angelic aircraft described thousands of years ago in the Old testament." Graham further contends that the reason UFOs are able to defy the laws of aerodynamics, is because the beings who operate these "celestial wonders" are non flesh-and-blood mortals, but instead are of a "higher order." He added that the UFO pilots—or angels—are "so glorious and impressively beautiful as to stun and amaze men who witness their presence."

Dr. Joseph Jeffers, D.D., of St. James, Missouri, doesn't try to keep it a secret that he has seen UFOs several times, both in the waking state, as well as part of a vision. "In my latest vision of UFOs, I described the object as looking like a gyroscope with windows that appeared as eyes. The windows were telescopic to give the views (inside) a better look. In the book of the Bible, Ezekiel 1:18, it says, 'The four wheels had rims and they had spokes; and their rims were full of eyes round about.' Verse 19 goes even further: 'And when the living creatures went, the wheels went with them; and when the living creatures rose from the earth, the wheels rose.' This is taken from the Revised Standard version of the Bible. In the first and second chapters of Ezekiel, in my opinion, the great prophet was referring to a UFO and its occupants."

Dr. Frank E. Stranges, president, International Evangelism Crusades (Van Nuys, California) goes a giant step further, in that he professes to have actually met and conversed with a space being inside the Pentagon in Washington, while he was speaking in that city several years ago. Rev. Stranges noticed one peculiar thing about the extraterrestrial (who looked just as human as any one of us), HE HAD NO FINGERPRINTS. Asked why, the spaceman replied: "Fingerprints are a sign of fallen man. Fingerprints mark a man all through his life. On the planet where I come from, there is no crime and so there is no need for such identification."

The alien, who wore a business suit when Frank met with him, added his own belief in God: "A long time ago, God looked over onto this earth and saw that the wickedness of men was very great. God, being a God of love as well as a God of justice, took upon Himself the form of a man and was born of the virgin, Mary. He succeeded in bringing man a plan of redemption through His precious blood. Everywhere Jesus went, He was doing good. In the midst of all His goodness, kindness and love, He was falsely accused, mercilessly condemned, and nailed to a cross. Even though He healed the sick, cleansed the leper, and even raised the dead, none of this was taken into consideration. They crucified Him that came into this world to save sinners. And you ask him what do I think of

Jesus? I know that Jesus is the alpha and omega of yours and everyone's faith. He, today, has assumed His rightful position as the ruler of the universe and is preparing a place and a time for all who are called by His name to ascend far above the clouds to where His power and authority shall never again be disputed. I believe that Jesus is the wonder of wonders and changes not. No, not forever and forever."

Clearly words of a divine prophet as spoken by a man from another planet.

Recently, we have begun to see a marked increase in the number of letters from those who have had dreams or visions regarding the times we live in. There is a "gut feeling" among many that we are already in the "Last Days" spoken of in the Bible. Many of these seemingly inspired revelations deal with UFOs and their part in the events of the immediate future. The feeling is that UFOs somehow tie in with the "Second Coming" and the rapture in which deserving souls will be taken off this planet.

Some of the accounts we have heard are admittedly "utterly starting" in their implications, and all we can say is that such experiences seem to be increasing in frequency to the point where it would be hard to deny their validity.

Take, for example, the story told to me by a young man who had just arrived in New York from Africa. Just by accident, I struck up a conversation with him at a party. I was interested in knowing just how popular UFOs might be where he came from. "There's very little about them printed in the papers," he knowledged, "but people do talk about them in private, but only with those who share their sense of knowledge."

Since coming to the United States, the young man began to have a series of odd dreams that he only told me about because of the nature of our conversation. "Funny you should mention about UFOs," he smiled. "About two months ago, I woke up in a cold sweat. In my dream, I had heard all this noise down on the street, and from my left window, I could see cars jamming the intersection as far as the eye could see. I took the elevator downstairs to see what was going on. The sidewalks were packed with people pushing each other, as if in a mad scramble to get out of town. I tried to stop someone to find out what was happening, but I also got shoved aside."

The man said he got the distinct impression that the dream had something to do with Russia or China and a war. "Suddenly, the sky got brighter and, looking up, I saw this diamond-shaped object approaching over the tall buildings until it got closer and closer, eventually hovering overhead."

At this point, the dream always ends, but the dreamer feels that the UFO has arrived just in the nick of time as a friend and not a foe. "Why am I having this nightmare?," he wants to know. If it weren't important, it would not repeat itself so often.

Two different Canadians have recently written in with frightening nightmares they have repeatedly had. One of the readers (letter on file for verification) says that he was on the street in his dream, when these missiles shot overhead directed at twenty "target cities." He also observed a fleet of thirty cigar-shaped spaceships filling the sky. "I sensed that a high intelligence was in command and that they were sent by God." There was another episode in which "a large, heavy, dark cloud charged with bright, round nuclear fireballs contaminates everything to ground level."

Mr. Lorne Johnson of Sudbury, Ontario, says that he had a vision a long time ago that has struck in his mind. "In the vision I saw these ships—UFOs—in the air and the world was at war. When these objects came down a 'fear' came into all the soldiers and they stopped their killing. They saw that the weapons they were fighting with were small to what 'they' had, and it made them think they would all die if they did not stop the battle. In short, man knew he was doing wrong and he feared for his inner soul."

One of the most sensational letters of this nature I've

received came after an ad appeared in the *National Enquirer*. "Is there some way I can contact the author of *Psychic & UFO Revelations in the Last Days,* Donna S., of Sparks, Nevada, wanted to know, "because some of the statements in the ad for this book closely parallel a segment of dreams that came to me later in 1971."

Donna gives this fascinating narrative that covers a period of nine years: "In the fall, near sundown, I left my sister's house which sat only 300 yards or so from my own. I have no memory from that point on until I awoke in my own bed near daylight, terribly ill and with the strange sensation that I'd been spinning through cold air, hanging onto some sort of metal brace and feeling very scared.

"I kept a detailed diary of the dreams that were to follow, there were lists of things to do, a specific geographic diagram of a place I was to find and a special garden that I was to plant, harvest and preserve.

"It wasn't until seven years later that something else happened. This time it included my ten year old daughter who'd gone into town with me around ten in the morning. Neither one of us remember anything from the time I drove out of the driveway until nearly sundown that same night. We ended up in a town we'd never been to before, nearly 130 miles away.

"My husband thought I was going nuts not remembering what I'd done or where I'd gone, and so did our daughter. She developed a rash on her hair line that slowly spread over her scalp and neck. I developed severe swelling in my right arm that had to be operated on in November, 1979, and she had to be operated on for several lumps that wouldn't go away in her throat that December.

"Several months after that we moved to another state where we came across an offer to buy ten acres of land. The moment I saw it I knew it was the place in my dreams, the latitude, altitude, direction from the nearest town—it all matched.

"Later, I took out some drawings I'd made. It was as

149

though I'd stood on that very spot to draw them. It was then that I put my diary into manuscript form. Writing down every event as it had appeared to me and vividly described the very last week up to the very moment that the long silver ships with the thin red line on their sides, come down to collect the chosen.

"It was during the last week that the earth's crust began to crumble into itself and the air was thick with sulphur that rushed out of the ground, forming masses of greeenish, yellowish clouds, that the sun wouldn't penetrate for hours at a time.

"As the oceans seeped over the land, hundreds of thousands were dying everywhere. They played the last rites over and over again all over the world on every radio and TV station. I lived these things as if it had already happened."

So ends Donna's vision of peril, in which a certain number of people will be taken away by UFOs at the "last moment" just before the world destroys itself.

Far from the evil sorcerers of Satan, some have made the occupants of UFOs out to be, they are in reality, truly the "messengers of light," as the above clearly indicates illustrates. Instead of being fearful of them we should seek their help and advice.

Nightvisions

by Jim Girouard

In a vision in 1970, I saw myself standing outside at night at the foot of my bed, when in the distance appeared a shooting star and then another one, and then all the stars in the sky fell. I then looked up, and noticed a huge opening with red clouds around it, with light pouring from the opening, and inside was the infant Christ and then I saw buildings that formed the letters BBWWAATTCCHH on top. The changing letters then formed into BEWARE THE ANTICHRIST. At that moment an angel appeared and we talked a little, and then he placed his hand on my head and said "YOUR PROBLEMS WILL BE OVER SOON." I began to experience a blessing at this point, in the form of brilliant white light that permeated my entire being. I could see the light as well as feel it, as it pulsated and enveloped me totally.

Eleven years later, I had another night vision, this time in three parts that I have translated thusly:

1. The part of the stars falling from the sky has to do with a polar shift that occurs every 26,000 years. There is a passage in Revelation that refers to this. When the poles shift, it will be from east to west which it is now, to north to south. The stars will not necessarily fall from the sky. If you are standing outside at night when the shift occurs, it will appear as though the stars are falling, when in actuality, it is the earth which is moving.

2. This part concerns the opening and the infant Christ,

151

and the buildings.

The opening and the infant Christ signify the coming of a new kingdom of heaven on earth, which is yet to occur. The buildings signify ANTICHRIST which are organizations established by man, the dark forces, the powers of darkness.

3. The last and final part of the vision is about the angel and the revelation of light. This is definitely the most personal part of the whole experience and the translation for this part of it is peace, an inner peace that can only be recognized by direct experience. It is knowing that there is a guiding force that watches over you and protects.

For years I looked for an explanation of this experience. I started noticing a similarity between angels and extraterrestrials. So, for a long time I researched UFOs. I have been greatly influenced by an inventor by the name of Nikola Tesla. He seems to have this mental technique that is quite unique. I gave him some Tesla material to read awhile back, and what he does is he reads whatever he can on a certain subject and tries to first solve the problem in his head, and will later have a dream that reveals the solution. Right now, we are working on developing a wireless telephone system that Tesla invented and also used. I am encouraging you to consider converting over to Tesla's ideas. If you are not already familiar with his master plan which was never considered feasible in his time, but in realty was a true godsend to our technical problems.

This wireless telephone, for example, operates on a nine-volt battery and can transmit any distance by means of using the crust of the earth as a conductor. The device itself is called a transducer and costs less than a hundred dollars to build. Once in operation, both parties can communicate at a low cost rather than having enormous phone bills. If the corporation had listened to Tesla, there would be no more wars, no poverty. We would be as affluent as we were meant to be.

This means of conversion is within our grasp. We have a knowledge of physics and electricity. Parts can be obtained at stores like Radio Shack. It all has to do with the conversion of ideas. There is still enough time to convert.

I hope you get some inspiration from reading about my vision.

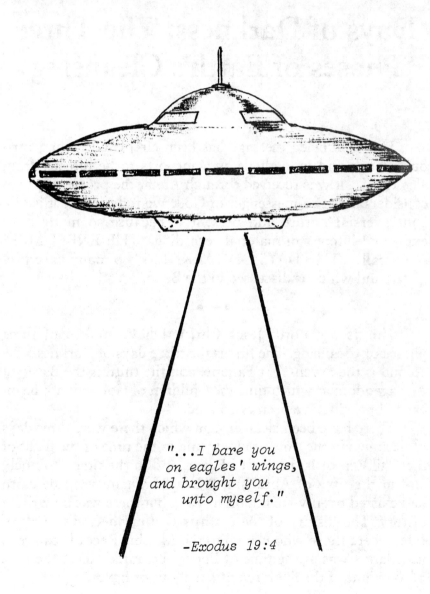

"...I bare you
on eagles' wings,
and brought you
unto myself."

—Exodus 19:4

Days of Darkness: The Three Phases of Earth's Cleansing

This channeled message has been circulated among various groups and individuals and purports to be directly from The Christ. It was received through Anna, the prophetess who considers herself a messenger of God. We fully realize it is of a controversial nature and present it because so many have expressed interest in material regarding "THE END TIMES" specifically "THE DAYS OF DARKNESS" so many have predicted and which is discussed in the Bible.

• • •

This is thy Lord, Jesus Christ. I have spoken of three phases of Cleansing. The first is the three days of Darkness; the second is the Seven-Year Famine; and the third is the Battle of Armageddon, at which time the Children of God will not be on earth, but will have been evacuated.

There have been cleansings in which there were three days of darkness in the time of Noah; and in the time of the flight of the Children of Israel out of Egypt; and in the time of Enoch; and in the time of Abraham. When Abraham was, the earth had existed twenty-six hundred years, but there was no written history. The history of the earth is written in God's Book of Life, where those who can go to the Akashic Records can read it. Atlantis was at the time of Enoch. Lemuria was at the time of the flight of the Children of Israel out of Egypt.

When ye see this writing, the time will be short before the beginning of the first cleansing. When the three days of darkness begin, it is well to think only thoughts of love and kindness to all that cross your mind. This will alleviate the pressure of unforgiven feelings. Those who are not able to cope with the hearing of these events are not yet right in their love relationship with God. When a person knows God is in charge of all things at all times, they can cope with anything God plans for them or the earth. They may be somewhat frightened, but will receive comfort and guidance by looking to God.

When the first Cleansing begins, it will be on a clear day in the middle of the day. The sun will fade away and darkness will begin to come over the land. There will be several hours before total darkness will be on all sides. There will be time for all enlightened to bring home their family; put water and feed outside for their animals and birds; and obtain supplies of food which does not need to be prepared and clean drinking water where it can be reached in the dark. Have warm clothing and bedding to remain wrapped in for the duration of the darkness, which will last three days. By the third night stars will be seen in the heavens. The fourth day the sun will shine again. During these three days of utter darkness, it is necessary that those in the houses do not look outside. It is necessary that they cover their windows with heavy covers which keep out the cold and keep the warmth inside.

The light that can be used for a short period of time has to be a battery-operated light. No fires or open flame light is to be used in the first three days. This will use up oxygen, which is already low in the atmosphere of the earth. Those who have respiratory problems will have a difficult time surviving. It is well if the door not be opened to anyone or for any reason. After the first three days, candles may still not be used for two more days; then ye can use any light or heat ye wish. Electricity should be re-established in a matter of time after the sun shines again. You can use whatever light or heat ye wish after the first

155

three days, but are required to stay inside your home another eleven days without opening the doors or looking out the windows. This is to know only that which is in thy house. The memory of the outside would not be easily removed.

The commodes should flush the entire time. The freezers will be off during the time the electricity is off. Food could be spoiled; test before eating. Not all those who are outside of God's care will leave the body. Some will live through it through sheer perseverance on their part—*the will to live*. This terrible thing must happen because the people have hardened their hearts. At the close of each age a cleansing is necessary. We are in the transitional period between the Piscean Age and the incoming Aquarian Age.

Those who will keep their animals inside to protect them will suffer the consequence of disobedience. God is not mocked. There is reason for what He asks of the people of the earth who have gone far astray from His laws. The animals are cared for by my beings, who are on earth for this reason. None will die. This cleansing is not for the animals or for little children. The little children who are left on earth without their parents are in God's care. The Angels will care for and comfort the little ones. There will very quickly be found loving homes for them to be raised in. The parents with little ones need not worry how they will be cared for. God's plan is complete.

After the three days of darkness are past, stay inside another eleven days. This is to reestablish the atmosphere on the earth and to give the Space Brothers sufficient time to take care of the debris the destruction has caused, and to remove the bodies of those who are no longer living. When the people come out of their houses on the fourteenth day, they will see no sign of the terrible things that happened. These will have been through a cleansing in their terrible experience, and will now accept God into their lives.

When the sun shines on the fourth day, those who are yet alive need to thank God. It is not better to be dead than alive

156

when God is carrying out a cleansing plan on the earth. When they are yet alive, they have yet an opportunity to establish a closer walk with God which will assure them a safer place in God's kingdom. By safer, I mean an area where God's laws are yet obeyed. After the three days of darkness and before the Battle of Armageddon, in a time when the people will wish to learn how to obey that which God has said they can do as the Lord Jesus Christ is able to do. When the aftermath of this terrible destruction is past, the world will then be in a famine for seven years. During these seven years the church and the school will be established with the help of Angelic guidance. In the time given for this activity, these lessons will be learned sufficiently that those who come back to earth will bring back the knowledge and the talents which they took with them. After that will follow the Battle of Armageddon. Those who are in God's care are not on earth during this time. They will have been taken up with me into a beautiful and peaceful area where they will stay until the aftermath of the last battle on earth is cleared away. Then chosen ones will be returned to earth the same way they were taken. This will be done by our Space Brothers and their spaceships. One phase will go directly into the next.. The Children of God will not be brought back until the debris of all the cleansing is cleared away and the earth is fresh and clean. The Children of God will have been in a state of heaven, and will have forgotten happenings on the earth. They will be taken with their bodies and brought back with their bodies. Nothing at all will be left on earth. Some things of this civilization will be found hundreds of years from now, or even thousands, and will be called "Artifacts of the Lost Civilization of Earth."

When the Children of God are returned again to earth, they will be beamed back asleep and will awaken on earth in an area close to where they were when they were taken up. They will not remember it but many will feel comfortable with their atmosphere, as if they had been there before. They will arrive in comfortable weather and will have nothing with them except some tools which the Space Brothers will leave with each adult. With these tools they will slowly begin to carve out a pattern for life. They will begin to plant seeds which will be left for them. They will carve dishes out of wood. They will build fires to keep warm and to cook food. They will find vegetables and fruit growing and seeds and nuts, and things which grew in the area when they were taken away. It will be much like the Garden of Eden.

The Children will have Angels and Space Brothers with them on earth to help them build homes; establish the various systems such as government, financial, educational, and the system in which people are made well when something affects them adversely. This will not be a medical system in which doctors use chemical and other harmful procedures for which they can charge an exorbitant price from the already impoverished patient or the patient's family. This healing system is called "The Well-Making by Mental Power." Each person will learn how to apply his own mental powers to all phases of his life. When a person is too ill to accomplish this, there will be practitioners who will help the patient heal himself by directing the patient's thoughts.

My thoughts will be picked up by all when I am giving them guidance or comfort. This they will have learned in the interim between the time they were taken and the time they are brought back.

When the Children of God come back they are no longer called by the name they had when they were taken. They will have forgotten. In time they will think of something to call each other. They cannot read or write now. The schools must teach this very soon. The angels will teach the teachers and build places to learn in.

There will be animals of other kinds; some were on earth before. There will be no vicious animals. All animals will love each other as people do.

The only supplies people will have will be those they can find around them. They will soon learn to make clothes to cover them up and keep them warm on cold nights. They will come back with the clothes they had on when they were taken. The weather will not be cold for some time—that is, until the people have learned to make clothes and bedding for themselves to protect them against the elements. Their God would not bring bad things upon them without giving them a way to protect themselves.

The Angels will have similar flesh bodies as they did at the time the Sons of God were upon the earth and found the daughters of man very fair, and loved them and had children with them. There will be children born of these attractions, who will be normal children. The fathers will disappear, one after another, when their work is done. The mothers of the children will know their husband was a Son of God and would be leaving again. They will raise the children with love and loving memories of their fathers. The children will be the same in all ways as are children on earth.

To get to this beautiful Garden of Eden with God and the Angels, one must now give his or her heart to God to be forgiven and Guided by God into a life of service to God.

Those returning will be much wiser and purer in mind and body. They are then given a piece of ground and tools to make their living and to learn to survive with the help of the Angels which God is sending with them to guide, guard, protect, comfort, and supply their needs.

The tools and other equipment are not of the earth kind. This is the age when God is ruling in the hearts and lives of those on earth. They will live closely with their Angels. The Angels will be protectors and companions to them. The people will have learned to communicate with God and with the Angels assigned to them by their Lord, Jesus Christ. The Angels are an ever-present help in all things.

Those who return to earth will have no recall of their families or homes. The healing work will have been done in them while they were in the area where they awaited return to earth. People of all ages will return.

Those who have family with them will stay with their kinfolk though they will not know they are kin. This will keep family love and ties between them. Those who are without family will be grouped in a way that they can soon become family. Their Angels will be a great help in this area. The Angels will express much love to them and create a feeling of togetherness by a bond.

Space Brothers are highly evolved Beings of great light who operate space vehicles to do the work which God requires in all areas of the Universe. They are involved with this very important work on earth. They live in their vehicles when they are not based doing clean-up work. They wear uniforms which resemble those of an army. The uniforms are not clothing; they are of a substance which is formed over the wearers. The Space Brothers do not have names except when they are assigned to a person or a group who can communicate with them, The name is relinquished when their work with that person or group is finished. The name is given to them by God and usually denotes a status. The spaceships also have names at that time.

The time is now when those who have the light of understanding need to heed this message and prepare the best they can. Where there is not enough money because of the economy to buy that which they need, and their heart is with God, they can count on their Angels providing that which they need. They will find they need less than they think. Their Angels have many ways to bring necessary things to them. In the wilderness the Children of israel were given quail when the Children were tired of spiritual food and were complaining loudly to God. Spiritual food is fruits and vegetables, nuts, seeds, honey, and grains. There was plenty of that for them. Before they left Egypt they were eating meat, and they thought they needed meat to have strength to travel.